Futurism

Severini: *The Blue Dancer.* (1912). Oil on canvas, with sequins, 24¹/₈ × 18¹/₄".
Collection Dr. Gianni Mattioli, Milan

JOSHUA C. TAYLOR

FUTURISM

The Museum of Modern Art, New York

Distributed by Doubleday & Company, Inc., Garden City, New York

Printed in Western Germany by Brüder Hartmann, Berlin
Published by The Museum of Modern Art,
11 West 53 Street, New York, May 1961
All Rights Reserved
Library of Congress Catalogue Card Number: 61–11271
Designed by Charles Oscar

Contents

page

Lenders to the Exhibition

Avv. Paride Accetti, Milan; The Estate of Vico Baer; Dr. Giuseppe Bergamini, Milan; On. Pietro Campilli, Rome; Mr. and Mrs. Sidney E. Cohn, New York; Dr. Giuseppe Cosmelli, Rome; Eric Estorick, London; Mr. and Mrs. Sidney Janis, New York; Dr. Emilio Jesi, Milan; Dr. Riccardo Jucker, Milan; Mr. and Mrs. Samuel F. Kurzman, New York; Dr. Paolo Marinotti, Milan; Dr. Gianni Mattioli, Milan; N. Richard Miller, New York; Mr. and Mrs. Morton G. Neumann, Chicago; Governor Nelson A. Rockefeller, New York; Mr. and Mrs. Herbert M. Rothschild, Ossining, New York; Mrs. Margarete Schultz, New York; Miss Barbara Jane Slifka, New York; Mr. and Mrs. Joseph Slifka, New York; Dr. Giuseppe Sprovieri, Rome; Miss May Walter, New York; Mr. and Mrs. Harry Lewis Winston, Birmingham, Michigan; Mr. and Mrs. S. J. Zacks, Toronto; Richard S. Zeisler, New York.

Musée des Beaux Arts, Grenoble; Gemeente Museum, The Hague; Civica Galleria d'Arte Moderna, Milan; Pinacoteca di Brera, Milan; Yale University Art Gallery, New Haven; The Metropolitan Museum of Art, New York; The Museum of Modern Art, New York; Musée National d'Art Moderne, Paris; Carnegie Institute, Pittsburgh; Galleria Nazionale d'Arte Moderna, Rome.

Richard Feigen Gallery, Chicago.

Collaborating Museums and Exhibition Dates

The Museum of Modern Art, New York	*May 31 – September 5, 1961*
The Detroit Institute of Arts	*October 18 – December 19, 1961*
Los Angeles County Museum	*January 14 – February 19, 1962*

Foreword

The Futurists were not only the first artists to take cognizance of the dynamism of a technological society, but they also produced works of art of extraordinary emotional impact. They translated the kinetic rhythms and the confused, intense sensations of modern life into potent visual form. The Futurists' approach to art, their manifestoes and demonstrations, set a pattern for many art movements which followed. The relationship between Cubism and Futurism, the impact of Futurism on Expressionism, and the sympathy between certain Futurist procedures and current endeavors are largely responsible for the growing interest in this movement, and the recent efforts to reassess its contribution as an artistic movement quite aside from its association with political and social events.

Launched in 1909 with fanfare by Marinetti, poet and lively editor of the controversial *Poesia*, Futurism—at first a literary movement—picked up momentum among the painters, who gradually evolved an art that matched the excitement of Marinetti's own poetic exuberance. By 1911 a type of painting clearly identifiable with the Futurist credo had taken shape. This book and the exhibition accompanying it commemorate the fiftieth anniversary of the epoch-making manifestation, *La Mostra d'Arte Libera*, in Milan in the spring of 1911, at which the positive direction taken by the Futurist painters was first to be seen.

From its inception Futurism was widely discussed in America as well as in Europe. Periodicals, Sunday supplements and little magazines were filled with reports and arguments about this new Italian movement. While the Futurists decided, as a group, not to participate in the Armory Show of 1913, they arranged a comprehensive exhibition of their work in 1915 at the San Francisco Panama-Pacific International Exposition. After the first World War many countries claimed movements under the Futurist banner; in fact, the terms "Futurism" and "Futuristic" became almost standard in popular references to avant-garde art. Yet the vital nucleus of the movement had spent itself, and the "First Futurism," as it is called in Italy to separate it from the politically associated "Second Futurism" of the 1920s and '30s, can be said actually to close with the first War. It is with this creative and innovating phase of the movement that this exhibition and book are concerned;

it seems felicitous that this exhibition, the first in the United States to present the whole range of the early movement, may help to focus attention upon one of Italy's most distinctive contributions to modern art, during the year in which the centennial of Italian unification is being widely celebrated.

Futurist painting and sculpture were, significantly, included in the Museum's exhibition *Cubism and Abstract Art* in 1936 and formed an essential aspect of the *Twentieth-Century Italian Art* show, organized by James Thrall Soby and Alfred H. Barr, Jr. in 1949. Today the Museum has the finest public collection of Futurist art, and we are happy to include sixteen important works from the Collection in this exhibition.

The Trustees of the participating museums wish to express their profound gratitude to Senator Giuseppe Medici, former Minister of Public Instruction of Italy, whose invitation to Professor Taylor, on behalf of the Italian Government, made possible this new study of Futurist sources; to Donna Benedetta Marinetti, who has preserved with care the vast documentation of Futurism made by Marinetti; to Donna Margherita Sarfatti, as well as to Avv. Carlo E. Accetti, youthful friend of Boccioni and Sant'Elia; to Dr. Giuseppe Sprovieri, who established the first permanent Futurist gallery in Rome in 1913; and to Maria Drudi Gambillo, co-editor of the indispensable *Archivi del Futurismo*. The recollections of Gino Severini, of Boccioni's gracious sister, Signora Boccioni-Callegari, of Signorina Luce Balla and Signorina Elica Balla, who have preserved their father's work with affection and respect, have contributed much.

To all the collectors, museum directors and dealers who have helped make this exhibition possible, we extend our sincere thanks, and we would like particularly to acknowledge the help of Mr. and Mrs. Harry Lewis Winston who, with great devotion to the Futurist artists, have created the most outstanding private collection of Futurist painting and sculpture outside of Italy, and who have lent to this exhibition with great generosity and have given invaluable advice and assistance. Dr. Gianni Mattioli, Dr. Emilio Jesi, Dr. Riccardo Jucker, Eric Estorick, and Mr. and Mrs. Herbert M. Rothschild have been most generous with loans from their excellent collections. Special thanks are also due to Dr. Umbro Apollonio, Curator of Historical Archives of Contemporary Art, Venice Biennale, and to Dr. Paolo Arrigoni, Director, Galleria d'Arte Moderna, Milan.

I am indebted to Marianne Martin who has furnished valuable information, especially as to the whereabouts of important paintings. The late Vico Baer, a close friend of Boccioni, before his death provided important personal recollections. Mr. Baer donated Boccioni's correspondence to the Museum's Library, enabling us to publish for the first time here a number of relevant letters. I wish to thank Margaret Scolari Barr for translating these letters, and Renée Neu for help in other Italian translations.

PETER SELZ
Director of the Exhibition

8

The Futurist Goal

With cries of "Burn the museums!" "Drain the canals of Venice!" and "Let's kill the moonlight!" the Futurist movement burst upon the consciousness of an astonished public in the years 1909–1910. For the first time artists breached the wall erected between conventional taste and new ideas in art by carrying their battle directly to the public with the noise and tactics of a political campaign. Taking their cue from the anarchists with whom as youths they were in sympathy, the self-styled Futurists published shocking manifestoes negating all past values, even art itself. Fighting their way towards a new liberty against apathy, nostalgia, and sentimentality, they became for a very wide public the symbol of all that was new, terrifying, and seemingly ridiculous in contemporary art. Newspapers throughout the world—in Tokyo, Chicago, London, Moscow—published snatches of their startling credo and accounts of their antics, with the result that—even before there was something distinguishable as Futurist painting—the term Futurism became a commonplace.

That so violently launched a movement should come out of Italy is not altogether surprising, for in no other country did the youth feel so completely subjugated to the past, deprived of a world of its own. The complacent Italian public was content with guarding a tradition and obstinately refused to notice new events in art and literature, at home or elsewhere.[1]

As for the term Futurism, there is no mystery about its origin, nor was it a word thrust by chance upon the artists as were "Impressionism," "Fauvism," and "Cubism." It was coined in the autumn of 1908 by the bilingual Italian poet, editor, and promoter of art, Filippo Tommaso Marinetti, to give ideological coherence to the advanced tendencies in poetry he was furthering in the controversial periodical, *Poesia*. He thought at first of calling it "Electricism," then "Dynamism," but in "Futurism" he recognized at once the word that would stir the minds of the hopeful young. The chosen term was announced to the world in an impassioned manifesto published on the front page of the respected Paris newspaper, *Le Figaro*, February 20, 1909. At the same time, hundreds of copies of the manifesto in Italian were mailed throughout Italy to people of importance.

Organized by Marinetti who was already noted for his declamation of

9

Caricature of a Futurist Presentation, from *Uno, due e . . . tre*, June 17, 1911

poetry, the poets who rallied under the new banner (they included such writers as Aldo Palazzeschi, Paolo Buzzi, and Libero Altomare) staged a series of public assaults on the poetic sensibilities of the nostalgically inclined Italian audiences, shouting their manifesto and reading their surprising poetry in theaters from Trieste to Rome.

In February 1909, Carlo Carrà, Umberto Boccioni, and Luigi Russolo, met with Marinetti, who had heretofore given little thought to the visual arts, and proposed that painters also be included in the movement. With Marinetti's enthusiastic support the three young artists drew up a manifesto of their own which their friends Aroldo Bonzagni and Romolo Romani joined them in signing. Eventually Boccioni's close friend Gino Severini, who had been painting in Paris since 1906, also agreed to subscribe to the document. Initially published as a broadside by *Poesia*, the manifesto caused sufficient comment to make Romani and Bonzagni reconsider and withdraw. On the manifesto's "official" publication dated 11 February 1910, appeared instead the name of Giacomo Balla, the precise and systematic divisionist painter in Rome, teacher of both Severini and Boccioni. These five, Balla, Boccioni, Carrà, Russolo, and Severini, became "the Futurist painters."

Boccioni, Carrà, and Russolo took their place beside the poets in the tumultuous theatrical presentations (the "Manifesto of Futurist Painters" was first read from the stage of the Chiarella Theater in Turin, March 8, 1910), sharing with them the whistles, shouts, and open combat (to say nothing of barrages of rancid spaghetti and over-ripe fruit) with which their declarations met.

The public remembered chiefly the negative side of the Futurists' campaign—their denial of morality, of the rights of woman, of the sanctity of the past—but the artist had to concern himself with the positive bases of creativity. What was the nature of the new freedom? What did it mean for art? "Futurism," remarked Giovanni Papini, "has made people laugh, shout, and spit. Let's see if it can make them think."[2]

Because the Futurist painters early adapted to their own use some of the formal language of Cubism, their painting has often been considered a kind of speeded up version of that classically oriented movement. In spite of the obvious testimony of Futurist writing and, more significantly, the painting itself, critics have persisted in seeing Futurism as an analytical procedure like early Cubism, differing only in its aim to represent motion, a goal better realized in moving pictures. Balla's charming little dog on a leash has misled many in understanding the aims of Futurism.

Motion for the Futurist painter was not an objective fact to be analyzed, but simply a modern means for embodying a strong personal expression. As different as their procedures were, the Futurists came closer in their aims to the *Brücke* or, better, to Kandinsky and the *Blaue Reiter*, than to the Cubists. And in their iconoclasm and concern for the vagaries of the mind, they had not a little in common with Dada and the Surrealists.

The Modern Pegasus   Dieu véhément d'une race d'acier,
Automobile ivre d'espace,
qui piétines d'angoisse, les mors aux dents stridents . . .
MARINETTI, *A mon Pégasse (A l'Automobile de course)*[3]

Marinetti, in substituting a modern racing car for the classical winged symbol of poetry, set the pace for much that would follow in the Futurist movement. Not only did the automobile with its violently pulsing, noisy life typify the modern world, spawned on science and devoted to mechanical achievement, it stood as well for a staggering speed that surpassed in its power the wings of Pegasus. Yet in assuming the role of Pegasus the motorcar became more than a proof of physical achievement; it became the symbol of a new kind of spiritual transport. Marinetti was not belittling poetic imagination. He wished to rekindle it in modern terms.

"We choose to concentrate our attention on things in motion," wrote Severini, "because our modern sensibility is particularly qualified to grasp the idea of speed. Heavy powerful motorcars rushing through the streets of our cities, dancers reflected in the fairy ambiance of light and color, airplanes flying above the heads of the excited throng . . . These sources of emotion satisfy our sense of a lyric and dramatic universe, better than do two pears and an apple."[4]

Like many of their fellows elsewhere, the Italian Futurists were fighting the estrangement from the world, the lonely isolation of the individual that was not only the inheritance of the artist but a common threat to modern man. They rejected firmly the temptation to brood over man's plight, sentimentalizing over his helplessness in the way fashionable at the turn of the century. They turned against the Lombard tradition that encouraged a crepuscular sadness to invade the works of even the most methodical divisionists. With Nietzschean arrogance they despised the weak and the timid, the thoughtful or hesitant, and wished to feel themselves rash, audacious, and capable of infinite accomplishment. They wanted their art to restore to man a sense of daring, an assertive will rather than submissive acceptance, to break through the insulating shell of self by sheer force if need be. "We want to re-enter life," they wrote; and to them life meant action.

"Dynamism" was a magical word for the Futurists. It signified the difference between life and death, between participation in an evolving, expanding universe and withdrawal into an eddy of personal isolation. They looked upon the world with the same eager expectation as the Transcendentalists, but the world they saw was not the quieting realm of tree and sky; it was the world of modern science that triumphed over nature, promising always something new in its rapid development towards an undetermined end. Dynamism was at its heart. Theirs was a transcendentalism founded on a whole new universe. "We are the primitives of a new, completely transformed, sensibility," they boasted. The new sensibility accorded emotional value to a mechanized world.

11

Like Kandinsky, the Futurists initially found the key to their expression in the complex color of Impressionism. Rather than rebelling against the Impressionists as did the Cubists, they looked upon them, rather than on Cézanne, as the founders of modern art.[5] They agreed with them that no object, moving or still, can be seen in isolation, but absorbs its surroundings just as it contributes to them. The Futurists saw this interplay between object and environment, expressed by the Impressionists in their complex broken color, as a continuous reciprocal activity and wanted to make the action more patent by extending its influence to the very forms of the objects. They wished, further, to add to this complex relationship between an object and its surroundings the effect on the forms of actual motion in space, since to our perception movement changes the shape of an object quite as much as does light.

They looked upon all objects, in fact, whether a static bottle or a racing horse, as embodying two kinds of motion: that which tends to move in on itself, suggesting in its centripetal force the internal mass of an object; and that which moves outward into space mingling its rhythms with those of other objects and eventually merging with space itself. With Bergson they agreed that to the perception there is no such thing as a definite, isolated object. There are only intimations of objects within the continuous flux of color and form that we perceive. Boccioni's "line/force" was devised to express this shifting relationship between "objectivity" and constant change, depicting neither the object itself nor its motion, but a synthesized image of both.

This is not so irrational a procedure as it may sound. Our mind is characterized less by the images it stores than by its activity in shifting and reassociating the images, admitting at the same time constantly new material. In their compositions that seem to move and grow continuously, the Futurists were attempting to talk the mind's own language, exploiting the mind's capacity for association and sequential observation to produce a new aesthetic satisfaction consistent with their modern consciousness.

They noted further that we cannot isolate the impact of our various senses. Touch, sound, smell may mingle with sight to influence our emotional reaction. And then memory, that powerful and uncontrollable image-giver, makes its contribution. "To perceive," quoted Severini from Bergson, "is after all nothing more than an opportunity to remember."[6] This was the rich body of experience from which the Futurists drew their pictorial material.

In order to clarify the notion of what their revivified perception meant, the Futurists used all manner of images, many of which their detractors thought hilariously funny. "Our bodies enter into the divans on which we sit, and the divans enter into us; just as the tram going by enters the houses, and they in turn hurl themselves upon the tram and merge with

[Handwritten marginalia:]

AESTHETIC BASIS:

breakup of distinction bet. fig. and space. (Impressionism) reciprocal and evolving interchange of fig. and space. → inf. of surrounding environment upon him effect of motion upon him.

it." Distance, either of time or space, does not exist. "And sometimes on the cheek of the person to whom we are talking in the street we see the horse going by a long way off." Such examples served only to suggest the wide scope of perception which makes the world more real, more present. They were meant to turn attention towards experience rather than towards the external object.

From their vivid awareness of the complexity of perception sprang the Futurists' primary concept of dynamism. They found an equation between the activity of the outside world and the activity of the mind that released their imprisoned sense of self and gave them a new confidence in their creative powers.

In their "Technical Manifesto" they said their goal in organizing a painting was "to put the spectator in the center of the picture." But what they were hoping was that by making the spectator participate in the complex activity suggested by the forms, colors, and fragments of objects, they were allowing the painting to take effective possession of his mind. They might have said with equal justice, "we want to thrust the world into the mind of the spectator."

What they strove for was an *Einfühlung,* an empathy with the world of things, an identity between object and emotion that was becoming the key to a new art of forms. "We do not want to observe, dissect, and translate into images," wrote Boccioni in rejecting objective analysis as a basis for painting, "we identify ourselves with the thing, which is profoundly different."[7] "We Futurists," said Carrà, "strive with the force of intuition to insert ourselves into the midst of things in such a fashion that our 'self' forms a single complex with their identities."[8]

Such statements bring at once to mind the ideas of some of the German Expressionists; it is not surprising that Marc was strongly influenced by Futurist painting. But Marc strove for identification with the animal world, escaping the city with its mechanical innovations in which the Futurists took delight. In contrast to the Futurists, most of the German painters seem to have courted a more exotic or Bohemian world.

That a mystical identity should be sought not through contemplation but through action is hardly a new and wholly modern idea. In a surprising article of 1912, Auguste Joly compared the procedure to the practices of the primitive mystic in his Orphic rites, wrestling with the direct experience of the physical world to transcend it in the climax of the orgy.[9] The association is apt. There is something of the orgy in much of Futurist art, created in an effort to kindle magic in an unmysterious world. There is, moreover, the same insistence on primitive sensibility, on beginning with the personal and the known rather than the traditional and learned, that is always the starting point of the mystic. "To understand the new beauties of modern painting," they declared, "the soul must again become pure."

Giovanni Papini began a bitter article in January 1913 by listing five types: 13 the savage, the child, the delinquent, the insane, the genius.[10] "These," he told his readers, "are the last remains of primary and original man, of true man." Only these, who were outside the boundaries of "rational" society, could be looked to as inspiration for creativity. Only these could still respond wholly to the voice of intuition. Only they still enjoyed a unified perception.

With great faith in untutored genius, Carrà and Boccioni helped spark an extraordinary exhibition in Milan in the spring of 1911. Anyone with something original to say in a work of art was invited to exhibit: children, workmen, those who used only form and color, Impressionists, and "those who draw from their own sensibility and from nature a world of forms and colors that contrasts with reality but is in harmony with the mind." Significantly the freest and most daring paintings shown were those of the Futurists themselves.

"Hurrah! plus de contacte avec la terre immonde!"[11]

Although in their manifestoes the Futurists exalted mechanics and science, their paintings were rarely concerned with mechanical forms. Their words, not their painting, relate to the mechanized compositions of Léger. Inspired by the excitement of the new city, they translated their emotions in very human terms. They were forced to humanize the machine, rather than mechanize man, because underneath their ruthless pronouncements and praise of war was an intensely personal idealism. Only through the revivification of personal experience, through a new definition of self, could they triumph over a threatening world to reach a sublime spiritual peace.

In spite of their constant threat of chaos, at the core of each of their compositions, at the climax of every action, they sought an intuitive intimation of an ideal order. It was not a pre-established order, to be sure, nor were they willing to describe it in terms of a *Section d'Or* or other formal scheme. Only in the highest moment of activity did they sense it. But it existed none the less, always just beyond the reach of definition. Futurism was indeed an apt word to describe their confident search for that which lay always just ahead. At a time of cultivated cynicism they expressed an optimism that was looked upon as puerile by some, as a salvation by others.

Whether it is a *Cyclist* by Boccioni, one of Severini's *Expansion of Lights*, or a *Flight of Swifts* by Balla, the experience of continuous movement generated by the painting finds eventually a kind of resolution. The motion or interplay does not stop, yet at a given point we feel that we have reached the climax, the moment of maximum concentration in the picture. This is not the same as recognizing finally the architectural stability underlying the dislocations of a Cubist painting; we do not leave the work with a new assurance of formal law and order, first threatened and then reestablished. Instead we are boldly launched or cunningly enticed to set out on an un-

14

Balla: *The Stairway of Farewells.* (1908). Oil on canvas, 41¹/₂×41¹/₂″. Collection Mr. and Mrs. Harry Lewis Winston, Birmingham, Michigan

trackable path that fragments and expands to take us well beyond the limits of our normal movement, and we are thus released into a realm of ideal motion that escapes the checks and measures of our physical world. This release is the Futurist's moment of ecstacy, his contact with the "universal rhythm" that grants him the freedom of the superman ... *"dans l'Infini libérateur."*

[handwritten marginal note: ...mantic empathy > ...en to the point of ...max.]

15

Balla: *The Injection of Futurism.* (c. 1918). Oil on canvas, 31³/₄ × 45¹/₄". Collection Mr. and Mrs. Harry Lewis Winston, Birmingham, Michigan

The Futurist Achievement

To search for a "Futurist Style" in the work of the original Futurist painters is a fruitless activity. Although they often spoke of stylistic means in their manifestoes and articles—line/force, simultaneity, interpenetration of planes, etc.—these were just so many ways of getting at a content they believed important. Futurism did not grow out of the discovery of a new formal language; it cannot be discussed in the same terms as Cubism. Taking their cue from the audacious poets who had already gone well beyond the free verse of the French Symbolists, each artist sought creative liberty through whatever iconoclastic means seemed most effective to him.

Futurism was not a style but an impulse, an impulse that was translated into poetry, the visual arts, music, and eventually into politics. "Futurism is only the praise, or if you prefer, the exaltation of originality and of personality," Marinetti declared to an interviewer in 1911; "the rest is only argument, trumpeting, and blows of the fist."[12] The nature of the Futurist impulse in politics, it might be added, should not influence the assessment of its achievement in art.

When the "Manifesto of Futurist Painters" was defiantly proclaimed from the stage of the Politeama Chiarella in Turin on March 8, 1910, there was as yet nothing that could be distinguished as Futurist painting. The manifesto was only a bid for freedom, and the neglected artists singled out for praise were the quite unsensational divisionist painters Giovanni Segantini and Gaetano Previati, and the remarkable but impressionist sculptor, Medardo Rosso. Although the "Technical Manifesto" published on April 11, 1910 lays the groundwork for a new kind of painting, it also is written in the future tense: a setting forth of hopes and expectations rather than a defense of accomplishments. A Futurist painting had yet to be created.

There were two stylistic forces behind the painters who signed the manifestoes: the tradition of Italian divisionism (derived from the French Neo-Impressionists), and the international linear style of Art Nouveau which still persisted in Italy as it did elsewhere. The systematic division of color inspired by Seurat and Signac had a somewhat different consequence in Italy, however, than in the North. For one thing it was rarely separated

17

Balla: *Work*. 1902. Oil on canvas, 68³/₄ × 49¹/₄". Collection Mr. and Mrs. Harry Lewis Winston, Birmingham, Michigan

Balla: *Bankrupt.* 1902. Oil on canvas, 46½ × 63¼". Collection Dr. Giuseppe Cosmelli, Rome

from quite specific expressive ends. The brooding landscapes of Segantini and the emotive, lyrical compositions of Previati have little in common with the paintings of Signac and Cross. The North Italian divisionist painters never succeeded in being objective in their view of nature, nor could they become chiefly concerned with pattern. Nature in the delicate, haunting paintings of Victor Grubicy, for example, is always the reflection of a state of mind.

In the work of Giacomo Balla, also, who studied in his native Turin before spending some months in Paris in 1900, can always be detected an underlying but quite specific emotional suggestion. In the painting *Work* of 1902, and even more in *Bankrupt* of the same year, the directly evoked mood of the painting is attached to a wider human significance. In one, beyond the sombre nocturnal obscurity and the subtly reflected rays of the lamp, is the 19

Carrà: *The Horsemen of the Apocalypse.* 1908. Oil on canvas, 14¹/₄ × 37¹/₄″. Richard Feigen Gallery, Chicago

Previati: *Crucifixion.* Galleria Nazionale d'Arte Moderna, Rome

suggestion of the weary city laborer; in the other, the minutely described door hides the tragedy of a bankrupt, ignored by the children who thoughtlessly scribble on the sealed portal. Such pathos of incomprehension and isolation is a recurrent theme in Balla's early painting.

In this regard it is worth noting that Carlo Carrà's first successful composition (1908) depicted a melancholy pregnant woman being comforted by a friend. Carrà, too, had gone to Paris in 1900, to work on decorations for the international exposition; later he spent some time in London. He admired the paintings of Turner and Constable and the French Impressionists, but his youthful work shows little influence from them. In 1908 he became associated with the active organization in Milan, the *Famiglia Artistica,* and it was there that he showed his *Horsemen of the Apocalypse,* a translation of his sober views of the world into allegorical terms. Both the linear composition and the broken color owe much more to the Italian Previati than to the French; but the style is secondary to the ponderous subject matter.

Also Luigi Russolo, who had less formal training than the other painters in the group, began with such subjects as *The Triumph of Death, The Sleeping City* (in which the clouds become amorous writhing figures), and a strange symbolic portrait of Nietzsche. These were all carefully executed etchings which were shown in an exhibition at the *Famiglia Artistica* in March 1910, in which Boccioni, Carrà, and Bonzagni also participated. In his painting, on the other hand, Russolo also showed himself to be a well trained divisionist.

Severini: *Spring in Montmartre.* 1909. Oil on canvas, 28¹/₄×23⁵/₈″. Private collection, Paris

Boccioni: *Young Man in a Landscape*,
(1902). Gouache, 11⁷/₈ × 8¹/₂″.
Collection Mr. and Mrs. Harry Lewis
Winston, Birmingham, Michigan

Boccioni: *Mob Gathered Around
a Monument.* (1908). Ink, 14¹/₄ × 9¹/₂″.
Collection Mr. and Mrs. Harry Lewis
Winston, Birmingham, Michigan

Both Gino Severini and Umberto Boccioni, fascinated by divisionism, studied with Balla in Rome and got from him both a belief in a disciplined study of color and light, and an interest in lowly subjects. But Severini settled in Paris in 1906, and his charming *Spring in Montmartre* (page 21) from 1909 shows how completely in three years he had absorbed the taste of his new environment. The patterned composition harks back to Vuillard of an earlier date, and the mosaic-like strokes are closer to Signac than to Balla. Already he has put behind him the strong sentimental impulse of the others.

Boccioni, introspective, restless, ambitious, went through a troubled period of development. The romantic melancholy expressed in his little drawing of 1902 remained always in the background to conflict with his desire for action and social protest shown, for example, in the lively drawing of a crowd from 1908. In 1902 Boccioni left Rome to study the Impressionists in Paris; later, in 1904, he settled for some months in Russia with a family he had known in France. But the effect of this travel is hard to find in the works he painted in Padua between 1905 and 1907, and the Milanese paintings of 1908 and 1909.

His portrait of the sculptor Brocchi, painted in Padua about 1907, shows a complete command of Balla's divisionist technique, a fresh eye for composition—also inspired by Balla—and a willingness to distort form for his pictorial purposes. Similar qualities characterize his bold self portrait of 1908, in which the figure is pushed to one side and the space plunges back in a deep, eccentric perspective (page 24). Newly settled in the city, Boccioni included in the background a typical scene of the outskirts, using material which he often repeated in these years and which eventually led to his first major Futurist work, *The City Rises* (page 37).

But the illustrations Boccioni drew in 1908 for popular magazines in order to survive in the city, show that he still could think in terms of allegory, sentiment, and the free linear style of Art Nouveau.[13]

In the winter of 1909–1910, Boccioni discovered new possibilities in his divisionist studies. He began to let light eat into the forms, creating a much more dramatic interaction between color and light, and space and solid. His rhythmic contours gave way to complex planes of light and shade. Futurism did not at once suggest a new style to Boccioni, but encouraged a new boldness of execution and a more adventuresome exploration of effect. His richly colored and adroitly characterized portrait of Signora Maffi, *La Maestra di Scena*, was shown in Venice July 1910 as a Futurist painting. Its bold impressionism was the first step.

Severini: *The Boulevard.* (1910). Oil on canvas, 25^1/$_8$×36^1/$_8$″. Collection Eric Estorick, London

Boccioni: *Portrait of the Sculptor, Brocchi.* (1907). Oil on canvas, 41³/₄ × 49⁵/₈".
Collection Dr. Paolo Marinotti, Milan

Boccioni: *Young Woman Reading.*
(1909–10). Pencil, 18³/₈ × 13¹/₄". Collection
Mr. and Mrs. Harry Lewis Winston,
Birmingham, Michigan

Boccioni: *Self Portrait.* 1908. Oil on canvas, 27¹/₂ × 39³/₈".
Pinacoteca di Brera, Milan

The first heralded group showing of paintings under the Futurist banner took place within the context of the extraordinary jury-free exhibition that opened in Milan on April 30, 1911. Some of the paintings had been shown late in December at the "intimate" exhibition of the *Famiglia Artistica*, but this was the first exhibition in force. "If you don't want to cover yourself with shame, giving proof of ignominious intellectual apathy . . . hurry to intoxicate your spirit before *50 Futurist paintings*," they advertised. With pride they quoted the critic of the *Corriere della Sera*: "The maddest coloristic orgy, the most insane eccentricities, the most macabre fantasies, all of the drunken foolishness possible or imaginable."[14]

Since the publication of the "Technical Manifesto" in April 1910, the Futurists of Milan had worked hard to realize in paint what they so confidently had set forth in words. The various ideas in the manifesto, obviously suggested by different members, could hardly be embodied in one style of painting, and Carrà, Boccioni, and Russolo each worked in the direction that seemed most "Futurist" to him. Meanwhile Severini in Paris, having completed his intricately patterned painting, *The Boulevard* (page 23), set out in his own Futurist direction with a huge canvas of dancers and crowd, *The "Pan Pan" at the Monico*. Balla, in Rome, was quietly expanding his careful divisionism to create more dynamic relationships of light and color, already detectable in his *Street Light* of 1909 (page 26).

Russolo, the least gifted as a painter but one of the most thoughtful of the group, was fascinated with the possibility of combining responses of different senses in a painting. This synesthetic interest, so much a part of Symbolist poetry and the self-consciously decadent sensualism in France in the late 1880s, he early demonstrated in *Perfume*, in which color and shapes are meant to evoke a heady, langorous scent (page 27). In more strictly Futurist language was a huge painting completed for the exhibition, entitled simply *Music* (page 28). A dark violet musician seated at a keyboard, creates a music that spirals and radiates around him, illuminating variously colored masks that correspond to the differing moods of the music. He is shown in various positions as he plays, and the spiral design is continuous. It is a literally conceived work, in design like some of the drawings of Romolo Romani which take their cue from Art Nouveau, but it has its fascination as the masks seem to appear and disappear.

Carrà, who was probably responsible for many of the major technical points of the manifesto although the language is clearly Boccioni's, set himself an ambitious program. Possibly taking a suggestion from Libero Altomare's poem, "Swimming in the Tiber," recited by Marinetti with great effect at many Futurist presentations, he created a painting in which the forms and colors of the swimmers and the flowing water mingle in a single continuous pattern (page 29). In the manifesto it had been pointed out that

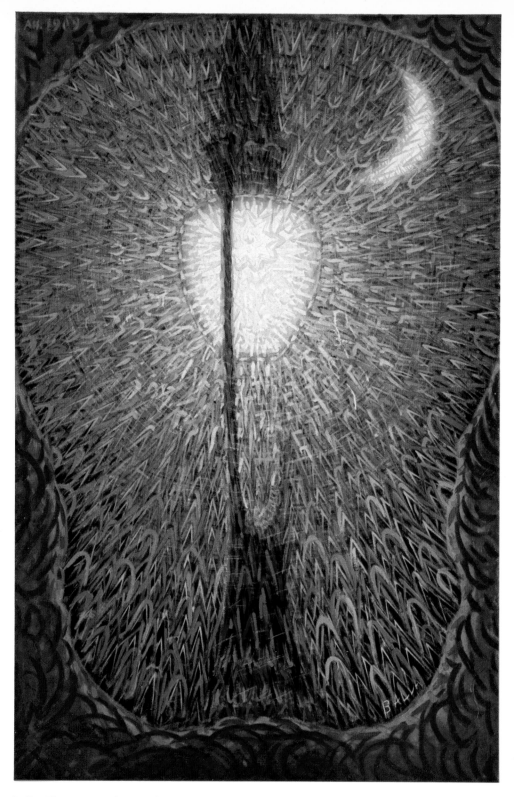

Balla: *The Street Light—Study of Light.* 1909. Oil on canvas 68³/₄×45¹/₄″.
The Museum of Modern Art, New York. Hillman Periodicals Fund

Russolo: *Perfume.* (1909–10). Oil on canvas, $25^{1}/_{2} \times 24^{3}/_{4}''$.
Collection Mr. and Mrs. Harry Lewis Winston, Birmingham, Michigan

Russolo: *Music.* 1911. Oil on canvas, 7′ 2″ × 55″. Collection Eric Estorick, London

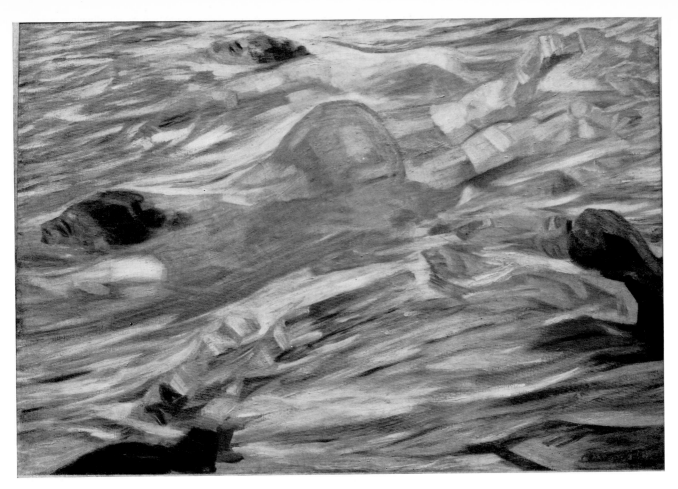

Carrà: *The Swimmers*. 1910. Oil on canvas, 41¹/₂ × 61¹/₄″. Carnegie Institute, Pittsburgh. Gift of G. David Thompson

Carrà: *Leaving the Theater.* (1910–11). Oil on canvas, $23^3/_4 \times 35^1/_2"$.
Collection Eric Estorick, London

there are two forces that tend to destroy the concreteness of form: light and motion. Carrà has demonstrated the idea in his painting in which the bright ripples of the water, the broad patches of divisionist color, break up the forms that are already made angular and elongated through motion. The painting as a whole, however, still relies on the persuasive continuous rhythm of Art Nouveau, luring the viewer to follow rather than to place himself in the midst of the scene.

This is less true of another painting from the period which does in a sense sweep the observer into space. This is *Leaving the Theater,* of which Carrà later remarked, "I believe that this canvas . . . is one of the paintings in which I best expressed the conception I then had of pictorial art."[15] The shadowy figures pushing out into the night, the diffuse form of the snow, the broken color, all help to break down the sense of a fixed point of view, creating instead the effect of an active rhythmic environment that surrounds the viewer. This, at least, is what Carrà was working towards, and what he achieved with notable success in his ambitious painting the *Funeral of the Anarchist Galli.* Here Carrà used stabbing rays of light interrupted by paths of abrupt action to paint a picture of "combat" rather than of men fighting. It suggests Marinetti's recommendation to the Futurist poets to use only the

Carrà: *Funeral of the Anarchist Galli.* (1910–11). Oil on canvas, 6' 6¼" × 8' 6". The Museum of Modern Art, New York. Acquired through the Lillie P. Bliss Bequest

text - (pp. 30-32)

infinitive of the verb so that the action would not be limited to a single agent: we are more aware of actions than of actors.

Carrà was remembering an unhappy incident he had witnessed some six years before. At the funeral of the anarchist Angelo Galli, who had been killed during the general strikes in Milan in 1904, a riot developed involving mounted policemen and the angry crowd. In the midst of the thrusting lances and flailing sticks, the red draped coffin was almost knocked from the shoulders of the pall bearers and trampled under foot. This is the moment that impressed itself on Carrà's memory and that now he recalled.

The principles underlying the composition are exactly those of the "Technical Manifesto." Arms multiply into a series of lines that describe the continuity of their action. So important, in fact, do these lines of motion become that they tend to dissolve the form of the arms themselves. Light, too, is transformed into visible energy, shining directly at us and breaking every area into active parts. "Everything moves, everything runs, everything rapidly evolves." Color, also, plays an active part. For all its fine divisionist strokes, the colors do not fuse; based on the contrast of complements rather than on graduated sequences, it sets up a struggle of its own. "Congenital complementary-ism is an absolute necessity in painting," the manifesto stated.

The interaction of light and the multiple images of motion creates an environment of activity hard to escape. Yet the activity does not belong specifically to any single figure. We identify ourselves instead with the activity as a whole and lose ourselves in it. Looking back on this picture, Carrà considered in the prime example of the declaration, "We will put the spectator in the center of the painting."[16]

Boccioni, too, was concerned with the evocation of action, but his painting went in quite a different direction from that of Carrà. Probably his first serious effort to embody the new hectic life of the Futurist in painting was his *Riot in the Galleria*.[17] The *Galleria* of Milan or, more precisely, the Restaurant Savini in the *Galleria*, was the regular meeting place of the avant-garde literary set and the Futurist painters. It was the beginning and ending point of most of their propaganda campaigns. Boccioni chose an environment he knew well and a situation not unfamiliar to an active Futurist.

But as personal as the situation may have been, the painting conveys little personal excitement. Its handsomely composed color scheme, the formal design of the impressive architecture painted with the precision of Balla, encourage us to view with some detachment the activity of the crowd. The figures seem suspended in motion as if caught by a waiting camera. Their excitement is not enough to force the walls to bend to their frantic rhythm or to shatter the steady light. The scene is active and fascinating, but we are not in the center of the action.

Boccioni later rethought the problem and, in April 1911, produced another tumultuous crowd scene, *The Raid*, in which, as the carefully dated drawings

Boccioni: *Riot in the Galleria.* (1910). Oil on canvas, 30×25¹/₄″. Collection Dr. Emilio Jesi, Milan

p. 32 -

Boccioni: *The Riot*. (1911). Oil on canvas, 19⁷/₈×19⁷/₈".
The Museum of Modern Art, New York. Given anonymously

Boccioni: Study, I, for *The Raid*. 1911. Ink.
Collection Donna Benedetta Marinetti, Rome

Boccioni: Study, II, for *The Raid*. 1911. Ink, 8×12".
Collection Donna Benedetta Marinetti, Rome

Boccioni: Study for *The City Rises*. (1910). Pencil, 5³/₈×7". Collection Mr. and Mrs. Harry Lewis Winston, Birmingham, Michigan

Boccioni: Study for *The City Rises*. (1910). Pencil, 5³/₄×8³/₄". Collection Mr. and Mrs. Harry Lewis Winston, Birmingham, Michigan

indicate (page 34), he attempted to draw the observer closer to the action. His method was closer to Carrà's. But somehow the viewer still remains outside.[18]

This cannot be said of a very large painting on which Boccioni began work probably in the summer of 1910. Ever since coming to Milan in 1908 he had made studies of the city. "I feel that I want to paint the new," he confided to his diary in March 1907 after a trip to the city, "the fruit of our industrial time. I am nauseated by old walls and old palaces, old motives, reminiscences ... I want the new, the expressive, the formidable."[19] He haunted the periphery where buildings were under construction and factories billowed smoke, and took particular pleasure in sketching the huge work horses which seemed to personify the harnessed force of the new industry.

He decided to bring together his various impressions into one work dedicated to labor. The growth of the composition was slow. At first he was content to assemble the horses and their drivers in a rather static plan. But as he worked, one huge horse began to assume the responsibility of all, pushing well past the center of the painting, dragging his driver with him (page 36). Next the buildings lost their static detachment and took on some of the push of the big horse; and light, exploding from the background, began to dissolve the individual forms. "I have tried for a great synthesis of labor, light, and movement," he wrote to the director of the Gallery of Modern Art in Venice.[20]

It is at this point in the painting, when the parts are shattered to obey the powerful rhythm of the whole, when light unites itself with physical action to make even the divisionist color a source of aggressive movement, that specific time and place lose their importance and we are caught up in an all-consuming action that seems universal in its implication (page 37). This was the dynamic abstraction toward which Boccioni was working. Different indeed from the painting by Carrà, Boccioni's *The City Rises*, as the painting was later called, overcomes the detachment of the viewer not by complexity of form but by sheer driving force.

At the same time Boccioni was evolving an image of staggering physical power, he was exploring a very different means of expression. Although the relentless activity of *The City Rises* typified one side of Boccioni's character —the side that drew him to the provocative activity of Marinetti—the brooding, emotional qualities he had shown as a young man were not easily suppressed. There was poetry to be found in aspects of life other than force.

Speaking of a painting on which he was working in the early autumn of 1910 he wrote:

"I hope it really will be the first of a long series of paintings that I want to do in which color becomes a sentiment and a music in itself ... If I am able (and I hope to be) the emotion will be produced with the least possible reference to the objects that brought it about. The ideal for me would be a painter who, wanting to evoke sleep, would not associate himself with the mind of the being (man, animal, etc.) sleeping, but would be able by means of lines and colors to evoke the *idea* of sleep, that is, universal sleep beyond the accidentality of time and place."[21]

35

Boccioni: Study for *The City Rises*. (1910–11). Oil on cardboard, 13×18¹/₂″.
Collection Dr. Gianni Mattioli, Milan

Boccioni: Study for *The City Rises*. (1910–11). Tempera on paper, 14¹/₈×23⁵/₈″.
Collection Dr. Emilio Jesi, Milan

Boccioni: *The City Rises.* (1910–11). Oil on canvas, 6′ 6¹/₂″ ×9′ 10¹/₂″. The Museum of Modern Art, New York. Mrs. Simon Guggenheim Fund

text - p. 35.

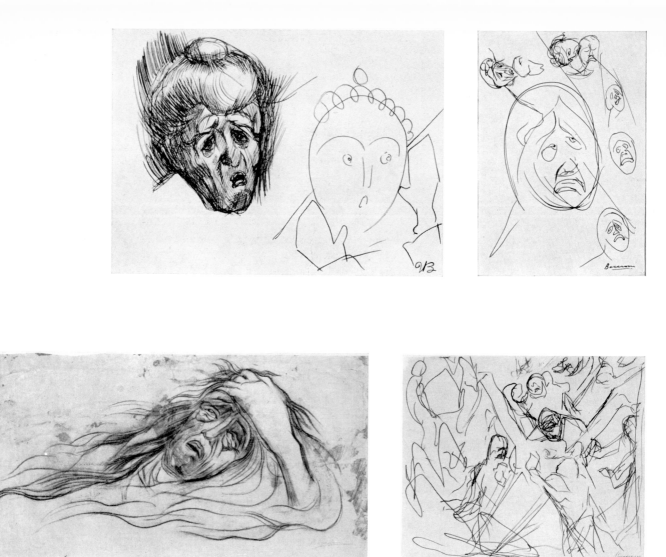

top left: Boccioni: Sketch for *Mourning*. (1910). Ink, 6¹/₂×8³/₈″.
Collection Mr. and Mrs. Harry Lewis Winston, Birmingham, Michigan

top right: Boccioni: Sketch for *Mourning*. (1910). Ink, 8¹/₈×5⁷/₈″.
Collection Mr. and Mrs. Harry Lewis Winston, Birmingham, Michigan

bottom left: Boccioni: Study for *Mourning*. (1910).
Pencil, charcoal and gouache, 9¹/₄×18¹/₂″.
Collection Mr. and Mrs. Harry Lewis Winston, Birmingham, Michigan

bottom right: Boccioni: Composition sketch for *Mourning*. (1910).
Ink, 6¹/₄×7¹/₂″. Collection Mr. and Mrs. Harry Lewis Winston,
Birmingham, Michigan

Boccioni: *Mourning.* (1910). Oil on canvas, 41¹/₂×53″. Collection Mrs. Margarete Schultz, New York

The studies for his painting *Mourning*, exhibited in December 1910, show him groping for such simple, expressive forms. Clearly with the model of Edvard Munch in mind (for example, his startling lithograph *The Cry*), he tried transforming literally rendered faces showing grief into diagrammatic masks that expressed the emotion directly and almost anonymously. The most elaborate study is a kind of compromise between the description of the face and the expressive rhythm of the line. The finished work is a haunting expression in strange color and disturbing form.

Another painting embodying a single emotion, even more elaborate and complex in organization, was shown for the first time in May 1911. *The*   39

Boccioni: *The Laugh.* (1911). Oil on canvas, $43^3/_8 \times 57^1/_4$". The Museum of Modern Art, New York. Gift of Mr. and Mrs. Herbert M. Rothschild

Text - p. 41

Laugh is a tribute to one of those bubbling and infectuous sounds that spreads from person to person, then group to group, until it seems eventually to convulse the entire atmosphere. *Mourning,* with its histrionic gestures, was a far easier and more conventional subject.

From the moment of their inceptions the two paintings were thought of in entirely different plastic terms. Instead of the elongated, angular, taut forms of *Mourning, The Laugh* began with full, rounded, floating lines, well epitomized in the plume of a fantastically large hat. The composition, like the sound, radiates from the plump untroubled face of the happy protagonist, pulling objects and people alike into its persuasive path. Doubtless these rolling, boisterous forms were much more in evidence in the painting when it was first shown than in its present form. Marinetti mentioned later in the year that the painting had been slashed by some unconvinced visitors to the Milan exhibition. Evidently Boccioni recreated the work on new canvas, taking the opportunity to add the angular forms and "cubist" bottles and glasses that have no place in the original sketches nor in carrying out his stated expressive theory. Probably the revised version was made late in 1911 after his return from a hasty viewing in Paris of the recent works of Picasso and Braque and his friend Severini.[22]

These paintings of Carrà, Russolo, and Boccioni at the "Free Exhibition of Art" in May 1911, showed the public that Futurist painting was more than invective and theory. It demonstrated, moreover, that painting could successfully undertake new problems of expression. Yet to the eyes of a man well schooled in the recent art of Paris, the attempts were weak and unsuccessful. Ardengo Soffici, painter and critic, damned the exhibition and was in turn set upon by the Futurists.[23] The encounter was fruitful: not only did it eventually bring Soffici and Giovanni Papini, his colleague on the lively Florentine periodical *La Voce,* to the support of Futurism, it spurred the painters to more critical judgments of their experiments in painting.

Boccioni: Composition sketch for *The Laugh.* (1911). Pencil, 4¹/₂×6″. Collection Mr. and Mrs. Harry Lewis Winston, Birmingham, Michigan

The Futurist Assault on Paris   *(February 1912)*

Having established an image of their work before the public of Milan, the Futurist painters set out on a more ambitious program. Marinetti made arrangements for an exhibition of their paintings in Paris during the coming winter and, aware of the significance of such an exhibition among the most advanced artists of the day, they became even more self-conscious about their procedures.

Again Boccioni was drawn in two opposing directions: towards the analysis of the world around him and his way of perceiving it, and towards the free expression of a state of mind. The first interest was encouraged by his contact with happenings in Paris, maintained through his close friend Severini and infrequent articles on the new tendencies.

41

Boccioni: *Study of a Woman Surrounded by Houses* (Ines). (1911). Oil on canvas, 53¹/₈ × 37″. Civica Galleria d'Arte Moderna, Milan

Boccioni: *The Noise of the Street Penetrates the House.* 1911. Oil on canvas.
Niedersächsische Landesgalerie, Hanover

The unusual painting of his friend Ines, *Study of a Woman Surrounded by Houses*, probably painted in the summer of 1911 and left unfinished, makes a distinct departure. Not only are the dislocated forms much bolder, but there is a greater openness to the composition. Abrupt straight lines take the place of continuous curves and melting surfaces. The eye moves freely back and forth and around, not pushed by a dominating force. The "dynamism" of the painting is generally diffused throughout the entire area.

So close in general spirit is the freely mounting composition of the painting to one of Delaunay's *Tour Eiffels*, reproduced in an article by Roger Allard that appeared at just this time, that it is hard to believe Boccioni was not impressed by it.[24] It was the hint he needed to escape the concept of motion in a painting as being limited to muscular activity. The difference, for example, between *Street Pavers* (page 44), doubtless painted at this time, and *The City Rises*, from not many months before, is enormous. The rhythm in the *Pavers* is traded back and forth amongst the figures, no single form pre-empts the center of attention, and the color spots are so large and sepa-

Boccioni: *Street Pavers.* (1911). Oil on canvas, 39³/₈ × 39³/₈". Collection Mr. and Mrs. Harry Lewis Winston, Birmingham, Michigan

Russolo: *Memories of a Night*. (1911). Oil on canvas, 39³/₄ × 39³/₈".
Collection Miss Barbara Jane Slifka, New York

rate that they seem to float in a world of their own. This tendency towards free construction built on angular lines and planes had been developing in Boccioni's drawings for some while. Only a slight suggestion was necessary to permit it to take over the paintings. As for color, some of the free studies of *The City Rises* show what an easy step it was from the divisionist color of that forceful painting to the open atmospheric color of the *Pavers*.

This was the moment also for Boccioni to demonstrate his conception of a painting of simultaneity. His *The Noise of the Street Penetrates the House* (page 43) is like opening a window on a noisy city: workmen climb ladders and shout, horses are everywhere, and the houses crowd around the viewer with the same mounting energy as in the *Woman Surrounded by Houses*. With a centripetal force it all crowds in at once upon the consciousness.[25]

Russolo, too, experimented with simultaneous images. In his *Memories of a Night* various events and unforgettable visions come together in a dream-like fusion. This quite different aspect of simultaneity is equally a part of

45

the Futurist conception. Not everything happening at once is synthesized, but a series of occurrences in time are juxtaposed in the memory. Russolo was careful to illustrate literally some Futurist statements: the horse with multiple legs, the horse appearing on the cheek of the woman, etc. But more important is the free, dream-like association that relates the composition of the painting more to a process of thought than to a process of vision. It is one more aspect of painting as a state of mind.

The exhibition in Paris would mark the first appearance of Severini with the group, and he too put forth a special effort. In his quiet way he had made contact with all of the new tendencies developing in French painting, yet had continued in his own direction. The charming, patchwork *Boulevard* was his first bold step. By then he had absorbed many of the formal preoccupations of his Paris fellows, and the geometrical breaking up of form seemed less a daring conquest for him than for his colleagues in Milan. But the Futurist interest in night life, in the simultaneous sight, sound, and motion of the crowded environment of the city appealed to him, and he turned his attention to it. His little painting, *The Modiste*, entangles light, reflections, forms in an active but poised interplay. There is none of that polemical force in Severini that had become a characteristic of the Milan group, but his paintings are no less original. His huge *The "Pan Pan" at the Monico* (now destroyed), which was one of the major works at the Paris exhibition and on which he had worked for over a year, is an extraordinary re-evocation of lively dance rhythms, noisy chatter, and snatches of music. It is a completely lyrical painting with none of the burden of social protest or violent emotion assumed by the work of Boccioni. In its purely lyrical quality lie both its strength and its weakness.

In a hasty trip to Italy where he met Carrà and Russolo for the first time, Severini saw the works of his fellow Futurists and was appalled that they so little resembled the paintings of his friends in Paris. Their resistance to principally formal preoccupations struck him as *retardataire*. Impressed by his criticism, Carrà and Boccioni (and possibly Russolo), with the aid of Marinetti, made a brief trip to Paris in the autumn of 1911 to see at first hand the most recent trends in painting.[26] Introduced to many artists by Severini and viewing hastily the *Salon d'Automne*, they saw much that impressed them. With many new ideas in mind, they hurried home to complete old and make new works for the Paris exhibition, more confident in their use of an international language.

Apollinaire reported in his chatty column of the *Mercure de France* on November 16, 1911, that Boccioni had told him a good deal about the aims of Futurism. "If I understood correctly," wrote the bemused Apollinaire, "...they are above all preoccupied with expressing sentiments, almost states of mind (that is an expression employed by M. Boccioni himself) and with expressing them in the strongest manner possible."

"So I have painted two canvases," Apollinaire reported Boccioni as saying,

46

Severini: *The Modiste.* (1910). Oil on canvas, $25^3/8 \times 18^7/8''$.
Collection Mr. and Mrs. Joseph Slifka, New York

Severini: *The Obsessive Dancer.* (1911). Oil on canvas $28^3/4 \times 21^5/8''$.
Collection Mr. and Mrs. Samuel F. Kurzman, New York

"one expressing departure, the other arrival ... To mark the difference in feeling I have not used in my painting of arrival a single line from the painting of departure."[27] Thus stated the idea does sound as puerile as Apollinaire thought it, but the works to which he referred are by no means simple. Boccioni had developed rather complete versions of his imposing triptych, *States of Mind*, before going to France, using the kind of free expressive forms that characterized *Mourning* and *The Laugh. The Farewells* was constructed of flame-like lines in which embracing couples were wafted like Paolo and Francesca. In *Those Who Stay*, persistent depressing vertical lines engulfed the vague forms of figures slumping off into the distance. In contrast, *Those Who Go* was marked by the clacking rhythm of a moving train; glimpses of fleeting houses and anxious faces barely escaped the mad rush of diagonal lines.

These expressive procedures did not change in the finished works, but contact with the Cubists gave Boccioni new insight on how complex a spatial organization could be without a loss of clarity. So he painted a new version of the triptych (pages 50—51) on his return from Paris, destroying all vagueness of form, giving his panels a new concreteness, far from the haze of impressionism. He glimpsed the possibility of a whole new vocabulary.

Boccioni: Study for *States of Mind: Those Who Stay*. (1911). Pencil, 23×34". The Museum of Modern Art, New York. Gift of Vico Baer

Boccioni: Drawing after *States of Mind: Those Who Stay*. (1912). Ink, 12³/₄×16³/₄". Collection Herbert and Nannette Rothschild, Ossining, New York

Boccioni: Study for *States of Mind:*
The Farewells. (1911). Pencil, 23×34″.
The Museum of Modern Art, New York.
Gift of Vico Baer

Boccioni: Study for *States of Mind: Those Who Go,*
(1911). Pencil, 23×34″. The Museum of Modern Art,
New York. Gift of Vico Baer

Boccioni: Drawing after *States of Mind:*
Those Who Go. (1912). Ink, 12¹/₂×16³/₄″.
Collection Mr. and Mrs. Harry Lewis Winston,
Birmingham, Michigan

Boccioni: *States of Mind: The Farewells.* (1911). Oil on canvas, 27³/₄ × 37⁷/₈". Collection Nelson A. Rockefeller, New York

comp. Monet. gare St. Lazar The new vocabulary, however, did not change the aim of the painting; *The Farewells,* for example, has an effect far different from a Cubist work. In spite of the angular parts, there is a constant rhythmic flow, welding images together and creating an expressive, emotional unity. The restless motion never stops, never reaches a point of stasis. Then too, objects, although treated summarily and reduced to geometric simplicity, have an insistent way of reclaiming their identity. The numbers are not a formal play as in the contemporary work of Picasso, but help bring to mind the train; the green swirls become embracing figures, and the superimposed straight lines suddenly identify themselves as railroad cars. Boccioni's subject matter is not to be escaped or pushed aside. The triptych retained its title: *States of Mind.*

Russolo, also emboldened by happenings in Paris, struck out in a new

Boccioni: *States of Mind: Those Who Stay.*
(1911). Tempera and oil on canvas, 27⁷/₈ × 37³/₄".
Collection Nelson A. Rockefeller, New York

Boccioni: *States of Mind: Those Who Go.*
(1911). Oil on canvas, 27⁷/₈ × 37³/₄". Collection
Nelson A. Rockefeller, New York

Russolo: *The Revolt.* (1911). Oil on canvas, 59" ×7′ 6¹/₂". Gemeente Museum, The Hague

direction not at all related to Cubism. His huge painting, *Revolt*, translates into geometric terms, almost the terms of a hieroglyph, the force expressed in such a painting as Boccioni's *The City Rises.* Russolo was a methodical artist, and once a pictorial problem was clear in his mind he proceeded to execute it with directness and simplicity. Here the houses are not distorted as if caught up in the passionate expression of the artist, but are simply tipped at an angle of forty-five degrees, thus becoming an arrow for the advancing wedge of the crowd. The painting has a sense of force, yet is painted with analytical detachment.

Of the three, Carrà was, at the moment, the most susceptible to the formal harmonies of Cubism. He was ready to turn his back for a while on matters of social conscience (his grim *Martyrs of Belfiore* simply disappeared from view) and devote himself to a more lyrical kind of painting. In *The Jolts of a Cab* and in *What the Streetcar Said to Me* he created free rhythmic images that mimic in their repetition and sudden dislocation of form, the erratic patterns of city noise. The sense of sound in these paintings is as important as in the dancers of Severini; the patterns cannot be explained by a scheme of visual analysis. Of the two, the *Streetcar*, with its sharp angles and blocky forms has more in common with Cubist painting, but its jerky movements that refuse to coalesce into a static unity mark its Futurist inspiration. Then too, in both, awareness of the situation represented is an essential

Carrà: *Jolts of a Cab*. (1911). Oil on canvas, 20⁵/₈×26¹/₂″. Collection Herbert and Nannette Rothschild, Ossining, New York

Carrà: *What the Streetcar Said to Me*. (1911). Oil on canvas, 20¹/₂×27″. Collection Dr. Giuseppe Bergamini, Milan

part of the painting; the works are at once directly expressive in form and evocative in subject.

Carrà's portrait of Marinetti and another painting shown in Paris, *The Woman with Absinthe*, come closest to the paintings of the Parisian Cubists. Yet here too the concept of the painting as a plastic rendering of a state of mind takes precedence over the play of forms. Although the portrait is now much altered (an inscription was added later by Marinetti himself), the poet still looks hypnotically from the canvas, suspended among the swinging planes of light and space.

The paintings shown, then, at the gallery of Bernheim-Jeune from February 5 to 24, 1912, were not all created in innocence, far from the influence of Paris. But in their essence they made a startling contrast with the evident trend in Parisian painting. Cubism tended to move away from significant subject matter, often using but a few simple objects in order that full attention might be paid to the formal transformation; color had been subjugated to other interests in the reaction to Impressionism and all it stood for; and the artists strove for ever greater discipline in the organization of form. Now a group of painters appeared who immersed themselves in subject matter—actually depending on it as a freeing force—reveled in the full sensuous range of Impressionist color, and substituted activity for form and excitement for contemplation.

Whether they wished to be or not—and the Italians were very irritating in their insistence on the originality of their purely Italian movement—the Paris painters were impressed. Grudgingly Apollinaire included in a rather disdainful article: "In fact the new art that is developing in France seems to have concerned itself with no more than the melody; the Futurists come to teach us, with their titles not with their works, that it could be elevated to a symphony."[28] The vigor with which the Futurists promoted the very ideas that were strangest at the moment to Paris, was hard to ignore.

So far as the public was concerned, newspapers throughout the world reported the exhibition, and illustrated articles on the movement, serious or mocking, became common Sunday supplement material. The *New York Sun* devoted a full page to the artists on February 25; on March 29 Margaret Hubbard Ayers explained to the readers of the *New York Evening Journal* that the "Futurist artists see through mental eyes"; and the *Literary Digest* published a feature article with illustrations. Great interest was shown in Japan, Greece, Denmark, Russia, and of course in Germany and England.

After its close in Paris, the exhibition moved to the Sackville Gallery in London (March), then to the Sturm Gallery in Berlin (April), and on to Brussels (June), The Hague (August), Amsterdam (September), and Munich (October). In Berlin most of the paintings were purchased by Dr. Borchardt (on terms that proved unfortunate for the artists), who continued to circulate the paintings. Beginning with the exhibition in Paris, Futurist painting took its place beside Futurist theory as an international force in art.

Carrà: *Portrait of Filippo Tommaso Marinetti.* (1911). Oil on canvas, 35³/₈×31¹/₂″.
Collection Donna Benedetta Marinetti, Rome

Soffici: *Displacement of the Planes of a Lamp.* (1912). Oil on canvas, $13^3/_4 \times 11^3/_4''$.
Collection Eric Estorick, London

Soffici: *Lines and Volumes of a Street.* (1912). Oil on
canvas, 20¹/₂ × 18¹/₂″. Collection Dr. Riccardo Jucker, Milan

Each in His Own Way   *(1912-1913)*

While their paintings were traveling through Europe and their manifestoes
were being read in many languages, the Futurist painters, now with more
mature vision and a clearer idea of what their painting could achieve, forged
ahead in their individual ways. While they borrowed each others words and
phrases to describe and defend what they were doing, they worked out their
own directions in painting.

   With the growing success abroad, not only young Italian painters but some
young intellectuals who had begun by doubting the creative capacity of the
noisy group, turned in their favor. After leaving *La Voce,* Giovanni Papini
and Ardengo Soffici initiated in Florence in January 1913 a lively periodical
that, to judge from its first editorial, was to be as bold as anything the Futurists had produced. *Lacerba,* as the review was called, eventually became
the principal outlet for Futurist manifestoes, combative articles, and the
texts written for delivery at Futurist manifestations but rarely heard in their
entirety. Soffici was a painter as well as critic and began to exhibit with the
group early in 1913, his rather soberly constructed paintings lending a new
note.

   For over a year, while the painters were diverging more and more, the
pages of *Lacerba* served to keep the ideological ends of Futurism in focus.

57

Balla: *Dynamism of a Dog on Leash (Leash in Motion)*. 1912. Oil on canvas, 35³/₄×43³/₈".
Collection General A. Conger Goodyear, New York

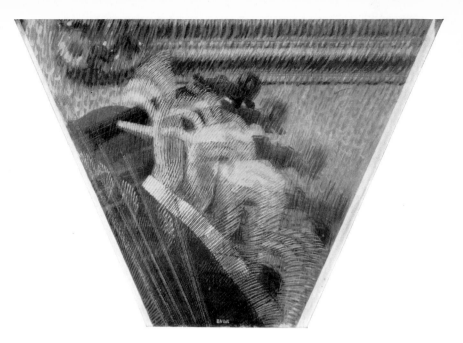

Balla: *Rhythm of the Violinist.* (1912).
Oil on canvas, 20¹/₂ × 29¹/₂″. Collection
Eric Estorick, London

GIACOMO BALLA

When the painters in Milan were rushing to complete works for the Paris
exhibition, Balla in Rome was quietly evolving his own ideas about the movement. Not of a nature to make hasty changes in the direction of his work, he
did not show his still-divisionist paintings in the initial Futurist exhibitions,
although one, *The Street Light,* was listed in the Bernheim-Jeune catalogue.
Only in 1912 did he take a really bold step in the direction of the others;
then he moved quickly.

Balla's scurrying little dog on a leash is probably the first Futurist painting
to display a genial sense of humor. "Dynamism" seems too formidable a
word to describe such a delightful pattern of rhythmic motions. It is dynamism subjected to the same sensitivity to pattern, precision of touch, and
subtlety of color to be found in Balla's earlier paintings. Not passion but acute
observation determined its forms, and the painter made no effort to suggest
that the dog was more than a dog or the leash more than a leash. The observer
is not thrust into an intense situation, but allowed to enjoy in detachment the
every-day lyric of a common scene. Yet the niceties of structure should not
be overlooked: the slight radiating diagonals, for example, that unobtru-
sively keep the forms in motion.

But Balla also was interested in bridging the gap between object and observer, with immersing the observer in the rhythmic experience of the painting.
The composition of his *Rhythm of the Violinist,* painted in Düsseldorf in 1912,

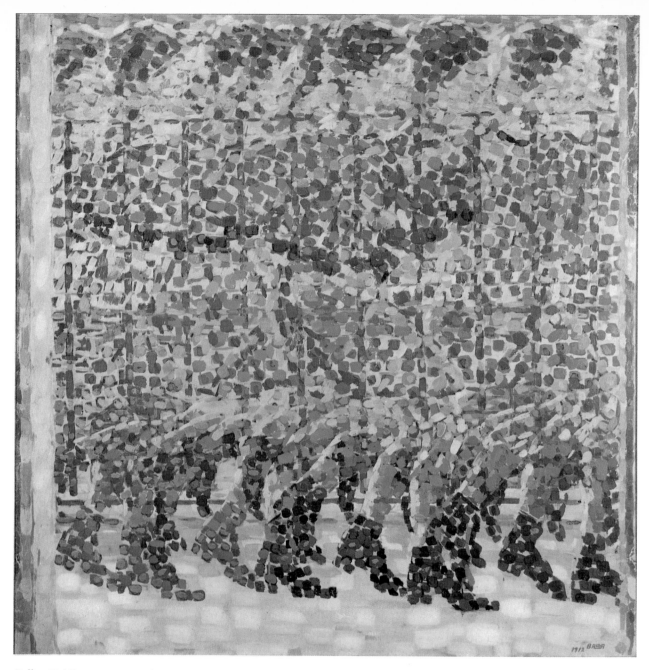

Balla: *Girl Running on a Balcony.* 1912. Oil on canvas, 49¼×49¼". Civica Galleria d'Arte Moderna, Milan. Grassi Collection

is built on stronger rhythms, and the moving forms fill the space as they dissolve one into the other.[29] The divisionist strokes are inseparable from the action of the forms, and color and form work together in creating an atmosphere of vibrant motion. But this painting devoted to music should not be confused in its purpose with paintings like Russolo's *Music* or Severini's cabaret scenes. Balla was a visual painter, and it was the movement of his violinist friend's hands that fascinated him. He chose not the forms that best suggest the tones of music, but those that recreate the activity of the violinist. Only through the vibrato of the musician do we sense the music.

As observers we come still closer to the enveloping activity of the painting in another analytical work of the same year. As with all of his paintings, this was the product of careful study and much thought. It brought together the continuous motions of a little girl running beside the railing of a balcony. Although he analyzed with care the successive images of the running girl, it is not this that gives the greatest sense of motion. The strokes of divisionist color are so large and distinct, and the combinations of color so shrewdly chosen, that they take on an activity of their own. In this active atmosphere the more literally represented movements of the girl assume not only a new sense of continuity but a more abstract quality of motion. The little running girl seems to have activated the sunlight and then been absorbed into its rhythm.

To speak of "activating sunlight" is not without point in considering the works of Balla. At the same moment he was working on *Rhythm of the Violinist*, he was experimenting with completely non-objective patterns of prismatic color to discover active harmonies in the components of light. He headed a letter to his family from Düsseldorf in 1912 with a little design of interlocking triangles of color and remarked: "First of all enjoy a moment this bit of iridescence because I am more than certain it will please you; this result is the product of an infinity of trials and retrials to discover finally in its simplicity the ends of delight."[30]

Balla painted many "iridescent interpenetrations," some large, some small, with dark colors and light, enjoying the various structures that seemed to emerge from the light itself (page 62). As Delaunay in his elusive series of "windows" from the same year, Balla invites the spectator to enjoy a period of escape in a weightless, luminous atmosphere. Such a quiet procedure hardly meets the requirements of Boccioni's will to force, yet it achieves in its own way the Futurist ends of identification and transcendence.

Above all Balla was devoted to essences: the essence of light or the essence of motion. Once he had freed himself from the rendering of solid objects, he found the possibilities enormous. In the innumerable studies of the flights of swifts that he worked on in 1913, he searched for the rhythmic form that would exactly embody the experience of their swooping course (page 63). The abstract form of their breath-taking speed was his goal; the flying bird was to lose itself in the path of its motion and the iridescence of light. Similarly,

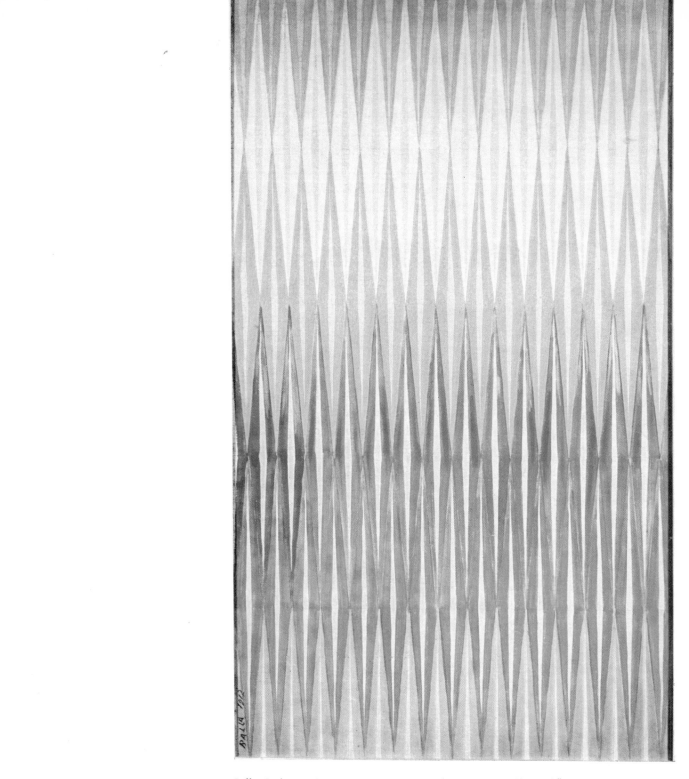

Balla: *Iridescent Interpenetration.* 1912. Oil on canvas, $39^3/_8 \times 23^5/_8''$.
Collection Mr. and Mrs. Harry Lewis Winston, Birmingham, Michigan

Balla: *Flight of Swifts.* 1913. Oil on canvas, $16^{1}/_{2} \times 20^{7}/_{8}''$.
Collection Hon. Pietro Campilli, Rome

Balla: *Swifts: Paths of Movement + Dynamic Sequences.* 1913. Oil on canvas, $38^{1}/_{8} \times 47^{1}/_{4}''$.
The Museum of Modern Art, New York. Purchase

Balla: *Abstract Speed—Wake of Speeding Automobile.* (1913).
Oil on canvas, 20¹/₈ × 25¹/₂″. Collection Hon. Pietro Campilli,
Rome

Balla: *Speed of an Automobile + Lights.* (1913). Oil on
cardboard, 19 × 26³/₄″. Collection Mr. and Mrs.
Morton G. Neumann, Chicago

his many studies of speeding automobiles reproduce few recognizable mechanical forms—and it is just as well since a 1913 automobile does not seem the essence of speed to the modern eye. The wheels have become spirals that expand into space, the forward motion becomes a succession of diagonals, light and the forms of surrounding buildings crowd in to oppose or re-enforce the action. The result is not a speed of thirty or sixty or a hundred miles an hour but, however modest the inspiration may have been, the utmost in speed for whoever looks at the painting. With his abstraction Balla was reaching for the universality his colleagues were insisting on.

The next step was to carry the consciousness of universal motion to the realm of the cosmic. Balla, interested in all scientific matters, was fascinated by astronomy, and the vision of the planet Mercury passing before the sun as it might be seen through a telescope served in 1914 as inspiration for one of his happiest series of paintings. Well beyond the motion of a motorcar and a long way from the charms of a scampering dog, this was an event of which the idea alone could carry this systematic, thoughtful artist to Marinetti's *"Infini libérateur,"* sought by the others in flashes of intuition and the exhaustion of violence. Caught up in the painting's broken spiral motion, the overlapping circles of transparent color, the piercing rays of light, the eye seems to lose itself in the vast spaces and complex order of an evolving universe. We are drawn into a great vortex that holds us, active yet suspended. It fits the image Marinetti had imagined:

> *je vole en souplesse*
> *sur la grisante plénitude*
> *des Astres ruissellants dans le grand lit du ciel!*[31]

Balla: *Mercury Passing Before the Sun as Seen Through a Telescope.* 1914.
Tempera on paper, 47¹/₄×39³/₈″. Collection Dr. Gianni Mattioli, Milan

Severini's most discussed painting at the Paris exhibition was the huge and lively *The "Pan Pan" at the Monico,* and he was quickly typed by his Paris associates as a painter of active café scenes. Actually his concentration on movement had hardly begun. Movement in the *"Pan Pan"* results chiefly from the sprightly, contrasting pattern, and the surprising dislocation of clearly recognizable parts. An ankle, the side of a face, a gesticulating hand that appears out of the lively chaos, are suggestive of rapid glimpses and shifting observation. The parts themselves contain little suggestion of action; they are simply linked in a manner suggesting time.

In a series of dancers he worked on after the exhibition, Severini developed a much more lyrical sense of form. At a time when the Cubists were becoming more rigidly geometrical, Severini, with his Futurist interests, became more fluid. The *Blue Dancer,* for example, with its swinging curves and eruptive angles, its rich variety of tone and glistening applied sequins, has a new lightness of spirit (frontispiece).[32] Significantly also, it is more the study of rhythms within the scope of a single figure than a contrast of movement between figures. The rustle of taffeta skirts and the click of heels are translated into forms that have in themselves a quality of motion. Severini convincingly evokes the dance without saying much about the dancer.

Similar in procedure but different in effect is the "second" dancer, the high-kicking *"chahutteuse."* The motion seeming to come from within the figure explodes with fantastic centrifugal force. We are drawn through space in a breathless, circular pattern, picking up hints of a foot, a ruffle, a lock of hair that confirm the figure yet hardly detain us in the madly continuing action. By combining the suggestion of abstract forms with identifiable parts, Severini invites us to experience, almost kinesthetically, the exhilarating action of the dancer. He has relinquished his interest in things as seen to concentrate on the action of pictorial forms themselves. A line or a sequence of color becomes an experience of motion which is then given particular meaning by the identifiable subject. Some months later, acknowledging his greater dependence on the forms themselves, Severini wrote, "It has been my aim while remaining within the domain of the plastic, to realize . . . forms which partake more and more of the abstract." It was his hope that, freed from the limitations of mass and time, painting "by means of abstract forms will give the pictorial rhythm of an ideal world."[33]

The most complex work in this transparent, rhythmic style is the large *Dynamic Hieroglyphic of the Bal Tabarin* (page 68), painted in Italy during the summer of 1912. The description "dynamic hieroglyph" accords with Severini's idea that the painting is first of all a synthesis of abstract rhythmic forms that attach themselves to other experiences through some means of association. Painted in the small town of Pienza, far from the gay Parisian night life it depicts, the painting's swirling rhythms enclose vividly remem-

Severini: *Second Dancer (White)*. (1912). Oil on canvas, 23⁵/₈×17³/₄″.
Collection Dr. Riccardo Jucker, Milan

Severini: *Dynamic Hieroglyphic of the Bal Tabarin.* (1912). Oil on canvas, with sequins, 63⅝×61½".
The Museum of Modern Art, New York. Acquired through the Lillie P. Bliss Bequest

bered bits of the far-off scene. A monocle flashes, the stiff frills of a red petticoat flash saucily from under the purple skirts, and bows, curls, and decorations become entangled in the general movement. Words stand out— the irregular POLKA and the smooth VALSE—to bring music to mind, and above the hubbub of conversation rise the words MICHETON and BOWLING. It is the synthesis in one complex and dynamic form—the "dynamic hieroglyph" —of a wide range of remembered experiences.

In order to prove, however, that he was not dependent on moving subjects, Severini also painted portraits. Most notable are the portrait of himself in a straw hat and the portraits of Mme M. S. (pages 70, 71). In these the same interaction as in the dancers takes place between the abstract rhythms of the forms and the dislocated fragments of identifiable things. Again it becomes clear that the Futurist painter was not trying to record the movements of objects, but to create a dynamic pattern of vision on the canvas itself; to make the viewer conscious of the dynamic aspects of his own experience.

Late in 1912 and early in 1913, Severini made several studies of a different sort: synthetic compositions of things seen on the Paris "Métro" and on an autobus. In *Nord-Sud* (page 72) with its jerky in-and-out motion, obtruding signs—which prove us victims of that bothersome habit of reading all print that comes before our eyes—function both for Cubist pattern and Futurist evocation.

The harsh and broken composition reflects an important tendency in Severini's painting at this time: towards a nearly complete abstraction of geometrically defined planes. Speaking of some abstract drawings exhibited in 1913 he said, "An overpowering need for abstraction has driven me to put on one side all realization of mass and of form in the sense of pictorial relief . . . Each drawing is an objective study, an effort in the direction of synthesis and the absolute. I consider the Plastic Absolute to be the communion, the sympathy which exists between ourselves [and] the center of things themselves."[34]

Out of this study developed Severini's interest in what he called the "plastic analogies of dynamism." Drawing largely on Marinetti's provocative "Technical Manifesto of Futurist Literature," he wrote a manifesto on the subject, which was not, however, published.[35] "Analogy," Marinetti had written, "is nothing more than the immense love that reunites distant things, apparently different and hostile . . . By means of vast analogies this orchestral style, at the same time polychrome, polyphonic, and polymorphic can embrace the life of matter." Severini believed that his "plastic absolute," which also wished to embrace the life of matter, was given particular value through this associative tendency of the mind.

Such a painting as *Dancer = Sea + Vase of Flowers* (page 73) might have first been inspired by the brilliant sun and sky over a sparkling sea. As the expanding rays of the sun mingled with the moving waves, the rhythms of a dancer with sparkling swirling skirts and waving arms came to mind. The

Severini: *Self Portrait.* (1912). Oil on canvas, 25¹/₄ × 21⁵/₈". Collection Dr. Giuseppe Sprovieri, Rome

Severini: *Portrait of Mme M. S.* (1912). Oil on canvas, 36¹/₄×25¹/₂″.
Collection Mr. and Mrs. S. J. Zacks, Toronto

Severini: *The "North-South" Métro (Nord-Sud)*. 1912. Oil on canvas, 19¹/₄ × 25¹/₄".
Collection Dr. Emilio Jesi, Milan

essential rhythmic image, interpreted in terms of expanding planes and prismatic color, would be much the same for the dancer as for the sea. Hence the title: *Dancer = Sea*. But once the painting was formed, a new suggestion arose, that of a blue vase with a bursting mass of brilliant flowers. So to the basic analogy is added the new overtone: *Dancer = Sea + Vase of Flowers*.

For Severini, his roots still firmly planted in the divisionist tradition, the prime source of energy in such images was light. But light, too, he now thought of as an abstract force expanding in space, linking all matter in its radial movement. It was the primary symbol of that energy which the Futurists felt activated all matter and which pushed out from its center with great centrifugal force or drew inwards to a dynamic vortex. Severini's *Spherical Expansion of Light* (page 74) is not an image of sea or dancer or bouquet of flowers, but the "plastic absolute" of light itself in its centrifugal radiation. The spectator is invited to enter into this primal image, to unite with a universal rhythm of nature that knows no boundaries and recognizes no isolation of mind or matter. It is an image even beyond analogy.

verini: *Dancer = Sea + Vase of Flowers*. (1913).
on canvas, with aluminum, 36¹/₄ × 23⁵/₈″. Collection
rbert and Nannette Rothschild, Ossining, New York

Severini: *Dancer = Sea*. (1913–14). Oil on canvas, with sequins, 36¹/₂ × 28³/₄″.
Collection Mr. and Mrs. Harry Lewis Winston, Birmingham, Michigan

Severini: *Spherical Expansion of Light (Centrifugal)*. (1914). Oil on canvas, 24³/₈×19⁵/₈".
Collection Dr. Riccardo Jucker, Milan

Although Carrà continued to write about Futurist ideals and the importance of dynamism (his polemical articles in *Lacerba* are well worth reading), his work moved steadily towards the simpler forms and stable composition more characteristic of the Cubists. The frenzied little red watercolor of a horseman, which translates quite literally that line from the Technical Manifesto "... a racing horse has not four legs, he has twenty, and their movements are triangular," is one of his few later efforts to achieve the effect of intensive action. More symptomatic of his new direction is *Rhythms of Objects* with its architectonic structure (page 76). Yet, although he uses the technique of vertical and horizontal lines similar to that developed by Picasso in late 1911, there is a restless movement in the painting that is distinctly non-Cubist. Even *The Galleria in Milan* (page 77), with its frankly Cubist planes and reduced color scheme, is clearly directed towards the creation of a sense of noisy ambiance rather than a monumentally stable design. The café sign "Biffi" takes

Carrà: *Horse and Rider.* (1912). Ink and watercolor, 10¹/₄ × 14¹/₄".
Collection Dr. Riccardo Jucker, Milan

Carrà: *Rhythms of Objects.* (c. 1912). Oil on canvas, 20¹/₈ × 26″. Collection Dr. Emilio Jesi, Milan

Carrà: *The Galleria in Milan.* (1912).
Oil on canvas, 36×20″.
Collection Dr. Gianni Mattioli, Milan

Carrà: *Study of a Female Nude.* 1912.
Brush and ink, 32¼×14¼".
Collection Dr. Emilio Jesi, Milan

Carrà: *Simultaneity (Woman on a Balcony).* (1912–13). Oil on canvas, 57⅞×52⅜".
Collection Dr. Riccardo Jucker, Milan

Carrà: *Boxer.* 1913. Ink, 23⁵/₈×19⁵/₈".
Collection Eric Estorick, London

Carrà: *Boxer.* 1913. Ink and ink wash,
⁵/₈×9¹/₈". Collection Mr. and Mrs. Joseph
Slifka, New York

its place in space, and the figures give a sense of scale to the towering mass of the walls and glass vaults. Through these points of reference the spectator can enter the picture, and the composition closes around him. While it does not threaten to explode with the force of a Boccioni, nor become all light and air like a Balla, it has none the less an excitement drawn from the modern city environment that agrees with the Futurist creed.

But Carrà was faced with a problem. Increasingly he wanted a sense of solidity and order in his painting, yet he did not want to fall into "archaism," the conventional compositional structure he accused the Cubists of using. He wanted, in other words, to attain Cubist order without sacrificing Futurist dynamism. It was probably late in 1912 that he began work towards this end on a series of studies of nude figures. He wrote to Soffici in April 1913, "I have found good plastic material in a female nude constructed with solidity without falling into archaism."[36] The subject seems strange for a Futurist, but Boccioni, too, at this time began a long series of figure studies. Subject matter was clearly becoming less decisive for the movement.

The bold brush strokes of Carrà's drawing of a nude woman, which relates to his painting, *Woman on a Balcony*, are certainly not lacking in force. Yet they counter one another in such a way that a sense of mass is created, a sense of solid form. Since the solidity is the product of actively opposing forces, however, which remain potentially free in space, the construction is within the Futurist concept of dynamic form. Action remains action, even though the effect of the whole is one of solidity. Rather less open but no less forceful in construction are the drawings of boxers produced early in 1913. But some of these retain a heaviness of modeling, a darkness that he eventually wished to escape.

His great achievement in this direction remains the "simultaneous" painting of the *Woman on a Balcony*. Painted in light silvery colors, so different from those of his earlier works, it has an elegance and poise quite new. "I wanted to combat in myself the *tendency towards tenebrism* as a necessity for the study of solidity," he wrote of this or of a similar painting in June 1913.[37] "I tried to achieve in the coloristic construction the solidity of certain light marbles and of certain white and ambered bones." He used also his theory of passive and active forms (the right-angle is the "cantus firmus" which supports the free activity of the other lines) to create an image that is momentary yet monumental, active and yet still.[38]

Using a language, a perception, entirely modern even in the Futurist sense, Carrà was already searching for the heroic poise and ageless quiet that he was beginning to admire once more in the work of Giotto and the fifteenth-century painters. He had explored the dynamism of his modern world, and now he wanted an order that lay beyond it.

While his fellows were searching for their own solutions to Futurist problems in painting, Russolo devoted more and more of his efforts to music. His new music, more audacious than the Futurist Pratella's, was composed not of traditional melodies or harmonies, but of carefully combined "unmusical" sounds. By admitting "noise" into the repertory of music, the range of experience could be expanded much as the "new sensibility" had expanded the expressive forms of painting. In March 1913 he published his manifesto "The Art of Noises" and in the next few years did relatively little painting, devoting himself to his elaborate machines, *Intonarumori* (Noise-organs), which produced on cue all manner of sounds, serving their composer much as the tape recorder serves some composers today.

In the intervening period, however, his painting did undergo change, growing in sophistication and clarity. *The Plastic Synthesis of the Actions of a Woman* (1912) is his own rhythmic interpretation of the Futurist dictum on motion. The movements of the individual figure multiply the initial image until it merges with the general abstract rhythm of the space. This treatment of space as if it too had positive rhythms, Russolo called expression of its "solidity." It suggests the capacity of space to assume an active role in relationship to solid form. In a sympathy between form and ambiance, not only is form rendered transparent and soluble, but space takes on positive shape and dimension, solid and void becoming thus equal in importance.

Russolo dramatized this equality of space and void in his *The Solidity of Fog* (page 82). Fog helps to make visible the dynamic form of space which interacts with the dynamic forms of the solids. He was willing to think of it in mystical terms: the merging rhythms symbolize the universal dynamism that pervades both man and his world.

In *Houses + Light + Sky* (which was exhibited in 1913 as *The Houses Continue into the Sky*), a similar idea is expressed in a different way: the solid forms of the houses reach out to assume dominance over space, transforming the environment in this way into a single rhythmic unity (page 83).

As in his earlier painting, Russolo was concerned with essential principles; in these works it was the all-pervading force that animates both man and his environment. Characteristically he stated his ideas in the most direct means possible.

Luigi Russolo with the *Intonarumori*

Russolo: *Plastic Synthesis of the Actions of a Woman*. 1912. Oil on canvas, 33$^{1}/_{2}$ × 25$^{1}/_{2}$″.
Musée des Beaux Arts, Grenoble

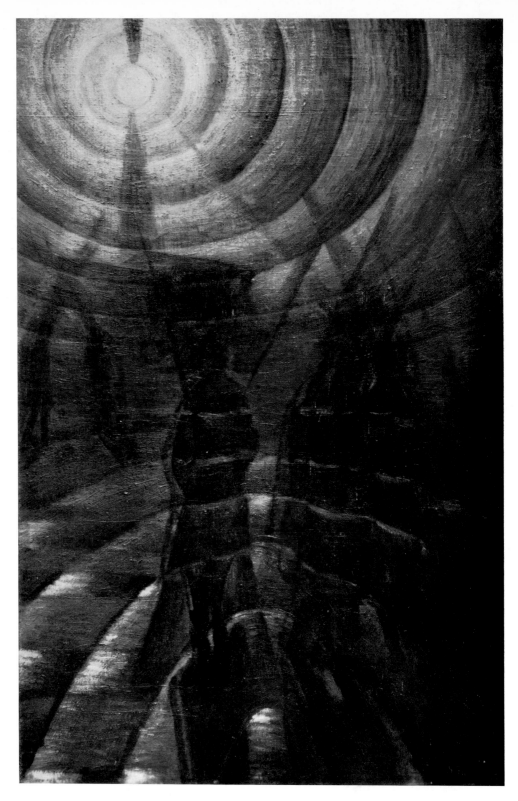

Russolo: *The Solidity of Fog.* 1912. Oil on canvas, 39^{1}/$_{4}$×25^{3}/$_{4}$″.
Collection Dr. Gianni Mattioli, Milan

Russolo: *Interpenetration of Houses + Light + Sky.* (1912). Oil on canvas, $39^3/8 \times 39^3/8''$.
Kunstmuseum, Basel

In the center of all Futurist activity, of course, was the restless Boccioni. Constantly doubting himself, yet constantly defending his position with exaggerated affirmations, he was continually in a state of creative ferment.

As a result of his contact with the Paris painters, early in 1912 he went through a period of interest in the intensive analysis of forms (page 86). A drawing of a man and woman at a table, which somewhat later served as the basis for a painting, has an angular, geometric quality new in its rigor to Boccioni's work.[39] This is true also of other analytical studies such as that of a bottle on a table or of one of his favorite subjects, a head seen against the bars of a window. He seemed determined to find a geometric basis for the relationship between the forms of objects, setting aside for a moment his belief in free intuition. ". . . Spiritualization will be obtained through pure mathematical values," he confidently wrote.[40]

But Boccioni could not long follow so rigid a pattern. He had somehow to link up this geometrical world with the world of flesh and muscular activity. This he did in a provocative, contradictory way in his huge painting, *Materia*. The looming image of his mother sitting immobile on a balcony, is broken into by the cubic forms of the houses that surround her, by the railing of the balcony, the form of the chair, and the angular rays of light that shine out from within the picture. In the midst of this formal interplay, the great gnarled hands maintain their quality as flesh, retaining contact with the palpable world. It is a majestic portrait, radiating a kind of internal natural strength that withstands the assault of a material world in flux. Yet such a contrast between the internal and external worlds is just what Boccioni wished to resolve. The external appearance of things and the internal spirit that animates them must become one. To express this, Boccioni, like his fellows, moved towards a greater abstraction. But it would no longer be a geometrical language since that had failed to penetrate to the internal vitality he wished to express.

In *Elasticity* planes seem to peel away from the forms, flowing gracefully into space (page 88). The horse and rider are not fragmented by an external light, but seem to dissolve in response to an internal force. The horse, for example, appears to have material substance, yet this we know only from the suggestions of the shifting planes. The limits of the form cannot be fixed. No longer do concrete objects resist the persuasive underlying movement; all is motion, and a sense of the object is given more through the nature of the action than through any suggestion of substance.

"The form/force," said Boccioni, "is, with its centrifugal direction, the potentiality of real form." To be alive, form must be seen as continually evolving. Each line and plane in the painting has the double function of establishing an object and creating a sense of motion beyond the object. It must become "the line that indicates the relationship between [the object's]

Boccioni: *Materia.* (1912). Oil on canvas, 7′ 4³/₄″ × 59¹/₄″. Collection Dr. Gianni Mattioli, Milan

Boccioni: *Couple at a Table*. Ink. Civica Raccolta delle Stampe
A. Bertarelli, Milan

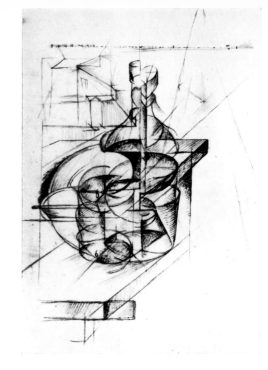

Boccioni: *Table + Bottle + Houses*. Pencil,
13¹/₈×9³/₈". Civica Raccolta delle Stampe
A. Bertarelli, Milan

Boccioni: *Fusion of a Head and a Window*.
Ink, 5³/₄×4³/₈". Collection Mr. and Mrs.
Harry Lewis Winston, Birmingham, Michigan

weight (quantity) and its expansion (quality)," to use Boccioni's terms.[41] In other words, the line represents exactly neither the form of the object nor the path of its movement or potential movement, but lies somewhere in between. It should be the unique line to express the continuity of a particular form as it extends in space.

This concept is well expressed in the drawing called *Muscular Dynamism* from early in 1913 (page 94), related to Boccioni's sculpture *Spiral Expansion* (now lost) and to *Unique Forms of Continuity in Space*. Undeniably it suggests a body in motion, yet it does not present a series of images like the successive exposures of a camera, nor just a blurred impression. The bold, forceful lines create both a sense of motion and an image of the body, without any one line's becoming only description or only a line of action. The drawing presents a new form, that of bodily motion made permanent and unchanging.

One step further towards the abstract is the powerful painting from 1913, *The Dynamism of a Soccer Player* (page 89). Although motion dominates to the almost total exclusion of physical mass, there is still a sense of muscular push that suggests at once a human agent. Yet, who is the player? The spectator is; there is no in-between personality on whom to foist the action.

Throughout this period of change, from early in 1912 to early in 1913, Boccioni was absorbed by a new interest in sculpture. It began in the spring of 1912 when he was in Paris, and he took occasion to see what was newest there amongst the sculptors. Teaming with ideas, he hastily published a manifesto on sculpture, dated 11 April 1912, even before he had seriously begun work in the medium. Yet his ideas were original and new, not simply borrowed from his Paris acquaintances.

If there was one primary influence on Boccioni's thoughts about sculpture it was the work of Medardo Rosso (page 90). Of all modern sculptors, only Rosso, in whose extraordinary works shadows and lights become sculptural forms and fleeting motions are sensitively sustained by the material, impressed Boccioni as having opened to sculpture a new field of expression. Only Rosso attempted "to render plastically the influence of an environment and the atmospheric ties that bound it to the subject." He was, none the less, an Impressionist, according to Boccioni, and did not take the liberating step that would free him from an art of appearances. Boccioni wished now to take that step.

Probably one of his first works was the *Antigrazioso*, the "anti-graceful" portrait of his mother (page 91). Combining the heavy sculptural mass with freely moving surface planes, Boccioni has created a lively image that seems to burst with inner life. It startlingly merges geometrical forms with soft fleshy shapes, yet is unified by the unflagging vitality of its surface. Many of Boccioni's cherished ideas find voice: the forms of far away houses merge with the form of the head; the face has an extraordinary range of expressions, it smiles, frowns, or is pensive according to the view and the viewer; and bold rhythms seem to envelope the physical form. Yet bold and expres- 87

Boccioni: *Elasticity.* (1912). Oil on canvas, 39³/₈ × 39³/₄″. Collection Dr. Riccardo Jucker, Milan

Boccioni: *Dynamism of a Soccer Player.* (1913). Oil on canvas, 6′ 5″ × 6′ 7″. Collection Mr. and Mrs. Sidney Janis, New York

Rosso: *Portrait of Yvette Guilbert.* (1897). Plaster.

Boccioni: *Anti-Graceful* (The Artist's Mother). (1912). Bronze, 23″ high. Collection Mr. and Mrs. Harry Lewis Winston, Birmingham, Michigan

Boccioni: *Development of a Bottle in Space.* (1912). Bronze, 15″ high. The Museum of Modern Art, New York. Aristide Maillol Fund

sive as the head may be—and it certainly shows at once Boccioni's impressive talent for sculpture—it is just one long step removed from the freely modeled heads of Rosso, relating to them rather the way the final version of the *States of Mind* related to the original studies.

Boccioni quickly applied to sculpture, however, the same determined analysis that characterized his early 1912 painting. Scorning traditional subjects, he concentrated on such material as the dramatic development of a bottle in space as seen in terms of its suggested dynamic force. Looked at as a source of motion the bottle becomes a complex dynamic form. Its roundness expands with a centrifugal momentum, engulfing the forms around it, while the highlights and shadows create counter rhythms that produce conflicting internal shapes. Observed from any angle the sculpture conveys a sense of motion; both light and motion are translated into positive sculptural forms.

As in painting, Boccioni initially wanted to create a kind of sculpture that would take into account the environment. The environment, however, must not be simply an Impressionist suggestion, as in Rosso, but an actual part of the construction. "We will break open the figure," he declared in his manifesto, "and enclose in it its environment." In his *Fusion of a Head and a Window* he did just that. The form of the head was cut through with a section of an actual wood and glass window, complete with metal catch. It was then further broken up with plastically rendered rays of light, gouged shadows, and sharply ridged highlights. Even more elaborate was *Head + House + Light*, a monumental sculpture based on the painting, *Materia* (page 85). Iron and wooden railings intruded on the figure, and plastically rendered light transformed whole areas of the form.[43]

But this sculpture was subject to the same difficulties as *Materia*: the figures seemed to be acted upon by outside forces rather than to be living parts of their environment. Only in the literal compilation of material was the sculpture "a bridge between the exterior plastic infinity and the interior plastic infinity . . ." In effect, it emphasized the difference between the living figure and the oppressive material surroundings. Addition was clearly not the road to synthesis.

"The problem of dynamism in sculpture," acknowledged Boccioni in the catalogue of his sculpture exhibition, which opened in Paris in June 1913, "does not depend, however, only on the diversity of materials, but principally on the interpretation of the form." Realizing this at some point in 1912, Boccioni started on his impressive series of striding figures, synthetic images of human motion, that culminated with his sculptural masterpiece, *Unique Forms of Continuity in Space*. Gradually he realized in sculpture as well as in painting how much a single form could stand for, and all contrivances and superfluous materials dropped away.

The figure in *Unique Forms of Continuity in Space* (page 95) strides forth, a symbol of vitality and strength, yet its impetuous step rests lightly on the ground as if the opposing air gave the figure wings. It is muscular without muscles, and massive without weight. The rhythms of its forms triumph over the limitations of the human stride to suggest unending movement into infinite space. Of all Futurist works this best illustrates Boccioni's often repeated term, "physical transcendentalism." The physical seems to lift itself by its own strength into the realm of the spirit. The long study of motion that preceded this work is justified not because it teaches us about perception or movement, but because it has produced an exhilarating symbol that in some mysterious way allows us to transcend for a moment those very physical qualities to which it draws our attention. Its forward thrust and assured pace express a buoyant optimism towards the modern world.

Having reached this impressive peak of lyrical expression in both painting and sculpture by mid-1913, Boccioni again subjected himself to a formal dis-

Boccioni: *Fusion of a Head and a Window.* (1912). Various materials. (Sculpture destroyed)

Boccioni: *Head + House + Light.* (1912). Various materials. (Sculpture destroyed)

Boccioni: *Muscular Dynamism.* (1913). Charcoal, 34×23¹/₄″. The Museum of Modern Art, New York. Purchase

opposite: Boccioni: *Unique Forms of Continuit* *in Space.* (1913). Bronze, 43¹/₂″ high. The Mus of Modern Art, New York. Acquired through Lillie P. Bliss Bequest

Boccioni: *Dynamism of a Cyclist*. (1913). Oil on canvas, $27^{1}/_{2} \times 37^{3}/_{8}''$. Collection Dr. Gianni Mattioli, Milan

cipline of renewed vigor. "Construction" became his key word, and his forms took on new abruptness and force. Selecting as a theme a racing bicyclist, he searched for those few forms that would best embody the intense muscular drive. The bicycle and rider become one coursing form to cut through space. The preliminary drawings range from quite literal descriptions to a few hasty lines, rendered in a wide variety of media and techniques. In the final painting, little is left of either bicycle or rider; only the irresistible thrust remains.

The thrust is made particularly telling in the *Cyclist* because it is so allied to the technique itself. The evanescent color and form of *Elasticity* and the *Soccer Player* are gone. In their place are bold slashes of strong color that add the gesture of the artist himself to the motion of the forms. Boccioni here

top left: Boccioni: Study for *Dynamism of a Cyclist.*
(1913). Ink, 8¹/₄×12¹/₈″. Civica Raccolta delle Stampe
A. Bertarelli, Milan

top right: Boccioni: Study for *Dynamism of a Cyclist.*
(1913). Ink and ink wash, 8¹/₄×12³/₈″. Yale University Art
Gallery, New Haven. Collection Société Anonyme

bottom left: Boccioni: Study for *Dynamism of a Cyclist.*
(1913). Ink and ink wash, 8¹/₈×12¹/₈″. Civica Raccolta
delle Stampe A. Bertarelli, Milan

bottom right: Boccioni: Study for *Dynamism of a Cyclist.*
(1913). Ink and tempera, 11¹/₂×15″. Civica Raccolta
delle Stampe A. Bertarelli, Milan

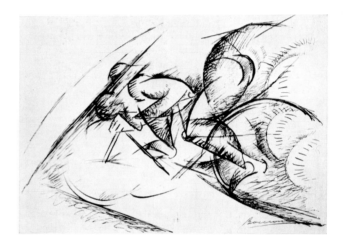

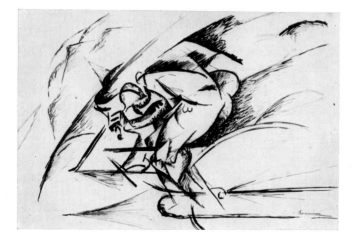

Boccioni: *I Want to Synthesize the Unique Forms of Continuity in Space.* Civica Raccolta delle Stampe A. Bertarelli, Milan

showed a new consciousness of the material surface of the painting.

The violent stroke, however, was also subjected to discipline in Boccioni's desire to fix his vital action in an unequivocally monumental form. *I Want to Fix the Human Form in Movement,* he labeled a series of twenty drawings of impressive boldness.[44] In his *Dynamism of a Human Body,* painted probably late in 1913, sober strength and unrelenting force substitute for grace and poetry. As if afraid of his own lyrical powers, Boccioni again concentrated on the *"antigrazioso"* (page 100). For inspiration he recalled Picasso's work from the period of *Les Demoiselles d'Avignon.* Evidently only in Picasso's painting of that period could he find the sober, uningratiating vision he felt need of.

Through this period of self-conscious construction ran another series of studies (pages 100, 101), somewhat related to those of the cyclist. Simultaneous images of galloping horses and rows of houses, they hark back in subject to *The City Rises.* But in the space of three years Boccioni's concept of pictorial language had basically changed. The motion is no less forceful in *Horse + Rider + Houses* (page 101), but is on an entirely different plane of experience. There is no suggestion of specific time or place, light no longer shoots its blinding rays across the forms, and no small figures pull back on the galloping horse. The motion is free and exists suspended in a space more readily described in terms of the imagination than of vision. Boccioni would characterize it as the realm of pure construction where all true art must reside.

To carry out his idea that the content of a work was expressed in the organization of the forms, Boccioni translated his *Horse + House* motif into a surprising piece of sculpture (page 101). Compounded of metal, wood, and cardboard, it no longer gave clear indication of its original subject. But it embodied in its composition the action distilled from many studies, magically infusing life into the obviously inanimate stuff of its structure.[45]

Boccioni: *Dynamism of a Human Body.* (1913–14). Oil on canvas, 39$^{1}/_{2}$ × 39$^{1}/_{2}$".
Civica Galleria d'Arte Moderna, Milan

Boccioni: *"Scomposizione" of the Head of a Woman.*
(1914). Tempera and collage on canvas, 13³/₄×13³/₄".
Civica Galleria d'Arte Moderna, Milan

Boccioni: *Head of a Woman* (Mother of the
Artist?). (1914). Pencil, ink, and wash,
12×9¹/₂". Collection Mr. and Mrs. Harry Lewis
Winston, Birmingham, Michigan

Boccioni: *Plastic Dynamism: Horse+Houses.* (1914).
Ink, watercolor, and gouache, 5¹/₄×8¹/₂".
Civica Raccolta delle Stampe A. Bertarelli, Milan

Boccioni: *Plastic Dynamism: Horse+Rider+Houses.* (1914).
Pencil, ink, and watercolor, 15¹/₄×22³/₈". Civica Raccolta delle
Stampe A. Bertarelli, Milan

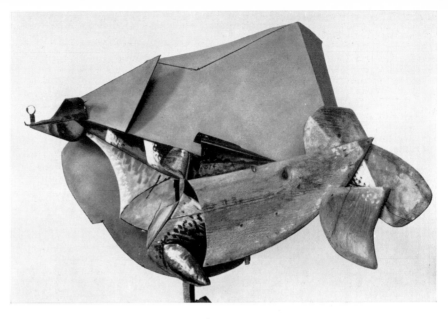

Boccioni: *Plastic Dynamism: Horse + Rider + Houses.* (1914).
Wood, cardboard, and metal. Peggy Guggenheim Collection, Venice

Boccioni: *Horse + Rider + Houses.* (1914). Oil on canvas, 41 × 52³/₄″. Galleria Nazionale
d'Arte Moderna, Rome

Giannattasio: *The Revolving Door of the Taverne de Paris.* (1913). Oil on canvas, 64¹/₂ × 74³/₄″.
Private collection, London

The Closing Years   *(1914-1915)*

Pushed by the ever-energetic Marinetti, the group activity of the Futurists continued at an increasing rate. Conferences were held, manifestoes published, and exhibitions of varying size and importance were organized in many parts of the world. Other artists, especially the young, were attracted by the activity and wished also to become Futurists, but for some time the original five guarded the membership jealously. However, at the First Free Futurist Exhibition, held at the Sprovieri Gallery in Rome from April 13 to May 25, 1914, many new artists were represented, including Sironi, Giannattasio, Prampolini, Depero, Morandi, and Rosai.

Mario Sironi was a close friend of Boccioni and Severini, and as early as

Sironi: *Self Portrait*. 1913. Oil on canvas, 20$^{1}/_{4}$×19$^{1}/_{4}$". Civica Galleria d'Arte Moderna, Milan

Sironi: *Composition with Propeller.* (1915). Tempera and collage on cardboard, 29⅜×24¼″. Collection Dr. Gianni Mattioli, Milan

Sironi: *Dancer.* (1916). Collage, oil, and various media on canvas, 30×21⅝″. Collection Dr. Riccardo Jucker, Milan

1913 expressed his complete sympathy with the movement. Officially he was admitted to the inner circle, however, only early in 1915. An introspective, solitary young man, his works had a haunting strangeness new to Futurism. In fact, his *Dancer* of 1916 seems more a comment on the emptiness of city night life, than a hearty endorsement of its newness and vigor. But the shattered images and relentless modernism of the Futurists were useful to Sironi in his search for expression.

Ottone Rosai was an eager exhibitor in 1914, finding in Futurism his first consciousness of formal order. Chiefly inspired by the painting of Soffici, which always remained close to Cubism, Rosai never felt easy with the full range of Futurist doctrine. His association with the movement was short-lived; even shorter was that of Giorgio Morandi who first showed at the free exhibition in Rome.

Prampolini and Depero were the beginning of the new order. They, with Balla, were to be the nucleus of the post-war Futurist movement in painting, and their influence, especially that of Prampolini, had wide effect in later Italian art.

Among those drawn to the movement at this time, of particular importance was a young man of twenty-six, introduced to Marinetti by Carrà in 1914. Antonio Sant'Elia was a young architect from Como, as yet with no substantial practice of his own. Sensible to the ferment created by the Futurists and aware of the new movements in architecture in other countries, he looked upon the immediate past and present of architecture in Italy with

Rosai: *The Carpenter's Bench.* (1914?). Oil and collage on cardbord, 18³/₄ × 27³/₄".
Collection Dr. Emilio Jesi, Milan

much the same attitude as the painters had looked upon the painting. In 1912 he had helped form a group of artists and architects at Milan which called itself simply, New Tendencies, and he contributed largely to the first exhibition of the group in May of 1914.

The foreword to the catalogue of the exhibition read much like a Futurist manifesto, damning the use of past styles and academic procedures. Architecture must, it said, make honest use of modern materials and suit modern needs. It should be audacious and bold, simple and calculated, making use of flexible, light, modern materials and avoiding the use of ponderous bulk as in past building. Rather than drawing its inspiration from nature, architecture should now look for inspiration to the new world of mechanics, "of which architecture should be the most beautiful expression, the most complete synthesis, the most efficacious artistic integration."

This statement, clearly drawing its form and even some of its language from Futurist doctrine, served as the basis for the actual "Manifesto of Futurist Architecture," signed by Sant'Elia with the date of 11 July 1914 and made public first in a broadside, then in the pages of *Lacerba* on August 10. The manifesto marked the young architect's official union with the movement of which he so evidently was a part.[46]

Besides a sharpening of the language in which the hand of Marinetti clearly shows, the manifesto differs in some few points from the earlier preface; one of the most significant is a new insistence that architecture be impermanent. HOUSES WILL NOT LAST AS LONG AS WE. EVERY GENERATION SHOULD BUILD ITS OWN CITY, it announced. While this is entirely in keeping with the Futurist notion that a creative art must deny its past, it is doubtful, considering the nature of his studies for monumental buildings, that Sant'Elia was wholly in accord. Yet his belief that architecture should make use always of the newest scientific knowledge would force an architect to condemn even his own earlier creations as obsolete. Building for obsolescence was for the Futurists a necessary premise for continued creativity.

Like the painters who knew what they wanted to paint before they had painted it, Sant'Elia's dream was projected into the future. Fascinated like the others with the modern city, he wished to recreate it in accordance with its own promise (pages 107, 108). Not the garden city of Howard but the *Cité Industrielle* of Garnier was his goal. "We must invent and remake the Futurist city to be like a huge tumultuous shipyard, agile, mobile, dynamic in all its parts; and the Futurist house to be like a gigantic machine." Elevators would be on the outside of buildings, buildings would be proportioned in accordance with their needs, and streets would be on several levels joined by escalators. Built of concrete, glass, and steel, they would proudly display their structure and mechanical functions.

Above all, said the new manifesto, embracing the poetic ideal of Marinetti, "in architecture the effort to harmonize, with freedom and great audacity, the environment with man must be understood; that is, to make the world of

Sant'Elia: *The New City.* (1914). Ink, 20⁷/₈×20¹/₂″. Musei Civici, Como

Sant'Elia: *The New City.* 1914. Ink, with watercolor, 12¹/₄×6⁷/₈″. Collection Avv. Paride Accetti, Milan

top left: Sant'Elia: *The New Station for Milan.*
Ink, 10⁵/₈×7¹/₂″. Musei Civici, Como

top right: Sant'Elia: *Dirigible Hangar.* 1913.
Ink, 9¹/₂×8⁷/₈″. Musei Civici, Como

right: Sant'Elia: *Architectural Dynamism.*
Ink, 10¹/₄×6¹/₄″. Musei Civici, Como

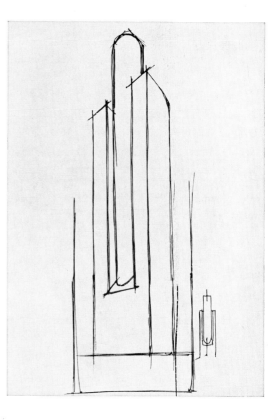

things a direct expression of the world of the spirit." Architecture gave promise of producing in reality what the Futurist painters achieved in symbol.

But so far as Sant'Elia was concerned, it remained a promise. His imaginative, vigorous sketches of soaring buildings and great hangars, of turbine stations and mechanized cities, served only to transmit his dream to others. Caught up in the war with the other Futurists, he was killed in action October 10, 1916.

In his provocative manifesto on literature published in May 1912, Marinetti had enunciated a poetical idea that eventually caught the imagination of the painters. Instead of "free verse" he now proposed "free words," *parole in libertà*. The word, freed from a limiting syntax, could communicate directly with the imagination, "the wireless imagination." Words were related by means of mathematical symbols, their organization on the page, or through special typography. They were, in effect, organized like evocative images in a painting, and the distinction between painting and poetry became hard to define.

"Free Words" made their entry into Futurist painting in the critical year of 1914, giving overt political voice to the active forms. An aggressive political outlook had characterized the group from the beginning. They had admired the persistent activity of the anarchists and learned much from them, but they chose as their particular cause the promotion of a more forceful Italian nationalism, to be demonstrated in a warlike attitude towards Austria. "We wish to glorify War—the only health giver of the world . . ." Marinetti had published in his original manifesto of 1909, and the cry was repeated in all of the noisy manifestations held by the poets and painters. When Italy declared war on Turkey over the possession of Libya in September 1911, Marinetti was delighted and went off to Tripoli to report on the situation. In the winter of 1912 he had a first hand view of the Balkan War and commemorated the experience in his first thoroughly Free-Word publication, *Zang Tumb Tumb*.

But until 1914 political agitation remained a secondary issue for most of the group; it was just one more way of inflaming the public and exalting action over passivity. Although motivated by a fierce nationalism, their aggressiveness was more poetic than political. With the first threat of a European war in 1914, however, the Futurists at once turned their hands to stirring up public sentiment. Boccioni and Russolo, in particular, joined Marinetti in planning public manifestations and publishing provocative statements against Austria. When war actually broke out in August, they insisted that Italy too must enter, looking to the war as a final awakening and unifying force. On August 15 *Lacerba*, with a new red masthead and the marks of heavy censorship, announced that it would henceforth devote itself wholly to politics, campaigning for intervention. As a result of their first major demonstration on September 16 in the *Galleria* of Milan (in which they burned several Austrian flags), Marinetti, Boccioni, and Russolo

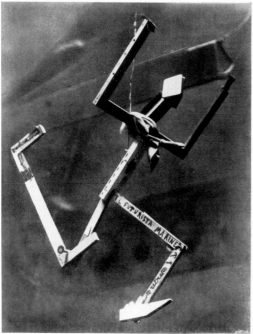

Marinetti: *Self Portrait*. From *Sketch*, London, May 13, 1914

Marinetti: *Parole in Libertà*

were imprisoned for some days and forbidden to take part in further public gatherings. But they found other ways to continue their activity.

Now that their artistic combativeness was associated with actual war, many of the Futurist painters forgot their will to abstraction and studied ways to draw the spectator not only into the center of the canvas but into the climate of battle as well. Their technique of the manifesto and their skill in composing forms came together in the use of Marinetti's Free Words.

The first of the painters to make use of the technique was Severini, whose drawing entitled *The Snake Dance* was reproduced in *Lacerba* on July 1, 1914. While this work is not specific in attaching political meaning to the excitement of mass demonstrations, it pointed the way to other of his works in which the association was made very clear.[47] Carrà's spinning collage, called *Patriotic Celebration*, published in *Lacerba* on August 1, just a few days before the declaration of war between Germany and the Allies, is a rousing work that seems to go off like a siren. It is a close fusion of painting and writing. Beginning in the center with EVVIVAAA L'ESERCITO and EEVVIIIVAAA IL REEE (Long live the Army! Long live the King!), it spirals outward with the HUHUHUHUHUHU of a siren and loses itself in echoes, shouts, songs, and the noise of traffic—TRRRRRR and traak tatatraaak.[48]

Another collage by Carrà, called *Pursuit*, is made up largely from news-

Carrà: *"Free-Word" Painting (Patriotic Celebration)*. (1914). Collage on cardboard, 15¹/₈ × 11³/₄".
Collection Dr. Gianni Mattioli, Milan

paper and program clippings listing sports and entertainments, that hem in the desperately galloping horse. Scattered letters seem to emerge with the hot breath of the straining animal, spelling out JOFFRE. Marshall Joffre had heroically succeeded in September in winning the hard fought battle of the Marne. In 1915 Carrà reproduced the collage in his book *Guerrapittura* (Warpainting) whose many Free-Word drawings all were devoted to the war.

Although Boccioni was among the most active as an interventionist, his paintings reflect less of the war than those of the others. His interest in Free Words he expressed in poetry, some of it published in *Lacerba;* but his paintings remained paintings, even when concerned with war-like themes. When he did use collage, however, as in the forceful *Cavalry Charge* (page 114) of late 1914, the bits of paper were chosen for their meaning, not only for their form. The clippings here tell of the war in France.

Balla created his own symbolic language for commenting on the war. Rather than words he used colors to make his expression concrete. The broken patch of red, white, and green (the colors of the Italian flag) suddenly gives new meaning to the great engulfing gray form in his *The Flag on the Altar of Its Country* (page 116). In a long series of works inspired by interventionist rallies and patriotic sentiments, swirling masses of the crowd dissolve into the rhythm of a shout or embrace the heroic billows of a flag. As usual,

Carrà: *Pursuit.* (1914). Collage and gouache, 15¼ × 26¾″. Collection Dr. Gianni Mattioli, Milan

Severini: *Flying over Reims.* (1915?).
Charcoal, 22³/₈ × 18⁵/₈″.
The Metropolitan Museum of Art, New York.
The Alfred Stieglitz Collection, 1949

Balla was looking for the most telling synthesis of forms in which to clothe the dramatic action.

With his tenacious belief in the suggestive power of abstract rhythms, Balla set out to create a symbol that would embody the aggressive action for which the group had always stood. Through the simple, carefully derived lines of his sculpture, *Boccioni's Fist* (page 117), he asserted in his own way the pugnacious force of Futurism.[49]

Finally in May of 1915 war became a reality for the Italians, and those able among the Futurists were with the first to volunteer. In July Boccioni, Russolo, Sant'Elia, Marinetti, and many younger associates became members of the volunteer cyclists. Sironi was already at the front.

In Paris, which he had reached late in 1914, ill and in desperate financial circumstances, Severini continued to respond to the war in his own way, 113

Boccioni: *The Cavalry Charge.* (1914). Tempera and collage on cardboard, 12⁷/₈×19¹/₂″.
Collection Dr. Riccardo Jucker, Milan

creating a series of drawings and paintings that bristle with the harsh lines and mechanical patterns of military matériel. As with the others, his interest in purely abstract suggestion waned. Yet in spite of the grim nature of the subject matter, Severini found a fresh, clean beauty in such unlikely objects as *The Armored Train.* He found new beauty also in the airplane, not because it was the symbol of speed, as it appealed to Marinetti and Balla, but because it afforded—actually and to the imagination—a new kaleidoscopic view of the earth. His *Flying over Reims* (page 113) is a happy mingling of new and old beauties. Many of these works were brought together for an exhibition in Paris in January 1916, which Severini boldly advertised as the "First Futurist Exhibition of Plastic Art of the War." But Severini's active adherence to Futurism was almost at an end.

In fact, the war for which the Futurists had campaigned proved the final blow to the "first Futurism." By the beginning of 1915 Carrà and Soffici had already broken away and were in search of an art more stable and more purely aesthetic.[50] Even Boccioni was showing signs of tiring of his youthful ecstasies; he began to discover a new satisfaction in the monumental com-

Severini: *The Armored Train.* (1915). Oil on canvas, 46×34¹/₂". Collection Richard S. Zeisler, New York

Balla: *The Flag on the Altar of Its Country.* 1915. Oil on canvas, 39³/₈ × 39³/₈". Collection Donna Benedetta Marinetti, Rome

Balla: *Boccioni's Fist—Lines of Force.* (1915). Cardboard and wood, painted red, 33″ high. Collection Mr. and Mrs. Harry Lewis Winston, Birmingham, Michigan

positions of Cézanne. There is already a hint of his new interest in *The Drinker* of 1914; it is confirmed in the massive, richly colored portrait of the composer and pianist Busoni painted while on leave from the army in 1916. But his new feeling about painting hardly had a chance to develop. On August 16, 1916, Boccioni, who had recently been recalled to active military service, was fatally injured in a riding accident; he died the following morning of August 17.

The first Futurism was a rhapsodic adventure of youth. Its drive towards an artistic ecstasy gave it the force of a new religion for those who were persuaded of its power. But it demanded of its adherents an intensity and blind faith that can only be expected of youth. Its very basis ordained its brief existence. None the less, the excitement it generated in Italy and abroad, whether expressed in anger, scorn, or open emulation, left a positive mark on almost every phase of modern art to follow.

Boccioni: *The Drinker*. (1914). Oil on canvas, 34¼ × 33⅞″.
Collection Dr. Riccardo Jucker, Milan

Notes to the Text

Note: Material cited that is to be found in the *Archivi del Futurismo*, edited by Maria Drudi Gambillo and Teresa Fiori (Rome: De Luca, 1958), is here referred to as in *Archivi*.

1 An exception was the Florentine periodical, *La Voce*, founded in 1908, which was an important force in encouraging rebellion against tradition and fostering the discussion of new ideas concerning society and the arts. Certainly the Futurists owed much to its renovating spirit.

2 "Il significato del Futurismo," *Lacerba*, I, 3 (1 Feb. 1913), 22.

3 Published initially in *Poesia*, I, 7 (1905), the poem was reprinted in *La ville charnelle*, 1908.

4 Introduction to the catalogue of Severini's exhibition at the Marlborough Gallery, London, April 1913. (*Archivi*, p. 115).

5 See Carrà, "Da Cézanne a noi Futuristi," *Lacerba*, I, 10 (15 May 1913), 99–101. (*Archivi*, pp. 160–163).

6 Introduction to the catalogue of Severini's exhibition, London, 1913. (*Archivi*, p. 113.) Bergson's writing was early known by Carrà, Severini, Soffici, and probably Boccioni. Sustaining Soffici's point (made in *La Voce*, III, 52 (28 Dec. 1911), 726) that the Cubists, especially Gleizes, Le Fauconnier, and Léger, did not at all express Bergson's concepts, Boccioni pointed out that the Futurists, on the other hand, did. ("Il dinamismo futurista e la pittura francese," *Lacerba*, I, 15 (1 Aug. 1913), 170). He earlier had quoted Bergson to support his theory of motion, in "Fondamento plastico della scultura e pittura futuriste," *Lacerba*, I, 6 (15 March 1913), 51–52. (*Archivi*, pp. 169; 144).

7 "Fondamento plastico . . .," *Lacerba*, I, 6 (15 March 1913), 52. (*Archivi*, p. 144).

8 "Piani plastici come espansione sferica nello spazio," *Lacerba*, I, 6 (15 March 1913), 54. (*Archivi*, p. 146).

9 "Le futurisme et la philosophie," *La Belgique artistique et littéraire*, July 1912. The bulk of this article was republished by the Futurists in a pamphlet with an Italian translation.

10 "Il giorno e la notte," *Lacerba*, I, 1 (1 Jan. 1913), 3. (*Archivi*, pp. 130–133). It is ironical that, under Papini's leadership, the Futurists should have so violently attacked Croce's aesthetic theory since, in their efforts to restore the importance of intuitive values, they shared much. Croce later criticized the Futurists, however, for hurling themselves too thoughtlessly at an abstract Utopian goal; they considered him too much a pedant. Carrà, however, recalled a sympathetic conversation with Croce at Naples in 1911. (*La mia vita*, p. 148).

11 Marinetti, "A mon Pégasse."

12 *Le Temps*, Paris, 14 March 1911. (*Archivi*, p. 473).

13 See, for example, "Allegoria del Natale," *Illustrazione Italiana*, XXXV, 52 (27 Dec. 1908), 617; his illustrations on pp. 486 and 521 of the same issue are, however, closer in style to his paintings.

14 From a broadside advertising the Futurist participation in the exhibition.

15 Carrà, *La mia vita*, p. 161.

16 *Ibid.*, pp. 73–74.

17 Possibly because of its confusing association with the dated drawings for *La Retata* from April 1911, this painting has sometimes been dated later. Its composition, however, is close to the illustrations of 1908, and its color is consistent with other works of 1910. Such a painting would seem hardly possible after *The City Rises* or Carrà's *Funeral of the Anarchist Galli*.

18 *The Raid (La Retata)* is in a Paris collection. The studies called *Baruffa* (Museum of Modern Art and Winston Collection), are a similar effort, probably dating shortly before this time.

19 Boccioni, *Opera completa*, p. 309. (*Archivi*, p. 225).

20 The revealing letters from Boccioni to Nino Barbantini, the progressive director of the Gallery of Modern Art, were published by Guido Perocco in the exhibition catalogue, *Primi espositori di Ca' Pesaro, 1908–1919*, Venice, 28 Aug.–19 Oct. 1958, pp. 114–120.

21 *Ibid.*, p. 116.

22 This hypothesis is further supported by the caricature of the painting in *Uno, due e . . . tre*, 17 June 1911, in which only the flowing circular lines are used to suggest its character (page 10).

23 "Arte libera e arte futurista," *La Voce*, III, 25 (22 June 1911), 597. There are many descriptions of the encounter between Soffici and the Futurists; for one see Carrà, *La mia vita*, pp. 149–151.

24 "Sur quelques peintres," *Les Marches du Sud-Ouest*, 2 (June 1911), 62. Also reproduced were works by Le Fauconnier, Gleizes, and Léger. Boccioni later referred to the article in "Il dinamismo futurista e la pittura francese," *Lacerba*, I, 15 (1 Aug. 1913), 170. Interestingly enough, Allard pointed out that Delaunay was following a Futurist principle (derived, certainly, from the manifestoes, not painting). This point is ably discussed by Maurizio Calvesi in "Il Futurismo di Boccioni: formazione e tempi," *Arte Antica e Moderna*, 2 (April–June 1958), 149–169.

25 The title of this painting, which dates probably from the

summer of 1911, and that of *Visioni Simultanee*, much more Cubist in form and doubtless painted after the trip to Paris, have sometimes been exchanged. Reproductions of the paintings in *The Sketch*, London, March 1912, together with the descriptions in the London catalogue, help in establishing the correct identity.

26 The trip to Paris is remembered very differently by Severini than by Carrà. Severini recalls Russolo as being there; Carrà does not. Certainly there is little direct evidence in Russolo's painting.

27 "Les Futuristes," *Le Petit Bleu*, Paris, 9 Feb. 1912. The relationship of Apollinaire to the Futurists is complicated. Obviously restive with the Cubist will to severe formal abstraction, he welcomed the fresh expressive subject matter and lyrical color of the Futurists. According to Severini he almost decided to use "Futurism" as the organizing term of his *Méditations Esthétiques* instead of "Cubism." But the nationalistic combativeness of the Futurists and Apollinaire's pride in Paris were not compatible. He lavished his attention instead on the Orphism of Delaunay and was roundly attacked by the Futurists for attributing their ideas to another. (See Boccioni, "I Futuristi plagiati nella Francia," *Lacerba*, I, 7 (1 April 1913), 99–101, in answer to Apollinaire's article in *Montjoie!*, 18 March 1913). Doubtless Apollinaire's theory was strongly influenced by Futurism; it is doubtful, however, if this aspect of Delaunay's painting owes much to the Italian painters. The controversy, which raged for some time, is discussed by M. Calvesi in "Il Futurismo e l'avanguardia europea," *La Biennale di Venezia*, IX, 36–37 (July–December 1960), 21–44.

28 Apollinaire, *Anecdotiques* (Paris: Gallimard, 1955), 49.

29 Sometime in 1912 Balla went to Düsseldorf for the first of three visits at the home of a former pupil, who had married a man with great interest in music. Balla was commissioned to decorate the music room and it was in the course of devising the decorations that he worked out his "interpenetrations." His patron, Dr. Loewenstein, served also as the model for the violinist.

30 In possession of the artist's family. Some of Balla's abstract works were published with a brief note by Ettore Colla, "Pittura e scultura astratta di Giacomo Balla," *Arti Visive*, 2 (Sept.–Oct. 1952).

31 "A mon Pégasse."

32 Severini recalls that his idea of using actual material on his paintings, such as sequins, grew out of a conversation with Apollinaire in which the poet remarked on the provocative effect the inclusion of real objects had in the works of some Italian primitives. He recalled, for example, the keys of Saint Peter in the painting by Crivelli in the Brera. *Tutta la vita*, p. 175.

33 Introduction to the catalogue of Severini's London exhibition, 1913.

34 *Ibid.*

35 See *Archivi*, pp. 76–80.

36 *Archivi*, p. 263.

37 *Ibid.*, p. 274.

38 Carrà's theory of composition at this time is described in his "Piani plastici come espansione sferica nello spazio," *Lacerba*, I, 6 (15 March 1913), 53–55. (*Archivi*, pp. 145–147).

39 The painting, freer in style than the drawing, was shown in Berlin in September 1913 and probably earlier in Rotterdam. It has sometimes been confused with *Figura di donna a tavola* from 1914, now in the Civica Galleria d'Arte Moderna in Milan, which was listed in 1916 as *Donna al caffè – compenetrazione di luci e piani*.

40 Letter to Barbantini, 12 February 1912. *Primi espositori di Ca' Pesaro*, p.118.

41 "Fondamento plastico . . . ," *Lacerba*, I, 6 (15 March 1913), 52. (*Archivi*, p. 144).

42 Although highly regarded by the young artists and well advertised by Soffici's perceptive articles, Medardo Rosso found little encouragement in Italy. For a perceptive early analysis of Boccioni's sculpture see Roberto Longhi, *Scultura Futurista: Boccioni*, (Florence: Libreria della Voce, 1914).

43 With the exception of the pieces represented in the exhibition and a reconstructed work in the collection of Peggy Guggenheim, Venice, all of Boccioni's sculpture was destroyed as the result of poor storage after the exhibition of 1916–17.

44 See drawing (now in the Raccolta delle stampe A. Bertarelli, Milan) reproduced in *Lacerba*, II, 6 (15 March 1914), 88.

45 This piece of sculpture of rather fragile construction has been much restored. This combination of materials, it should be noted, has little in common with the wood, metal, glass, etc. of his earlier works. Far from suggesting specific objective references, this diversity of material calls attention to the purely abstract nature of the work.

46 An academic argument has been carried on concerning Sant'Elia's tie with Futurism. The bibliography is summarized in *La Martinella*, Milan, XII, x (1958), 526–535.

47 A somewhat similar painting, *La Guerra*, is in the collection of Mr. and Mrs. Joseph Slifka. See letters from Carrà and Marinetti in *Archivi*, pp. 341–2. Apollinaire imitated some of the same sounds as Carrà in a "parole in libertà" published later the same year in *Les Soirées de Paris*, 1914, p. 387.

48 If the painters invaded poetry, the poets in their turn invaded the visual arts. In the early spring of 1914, Marinetti and Cangiullo began working with Balla on "object sculptures" in which various objects and materials were combined. Some of these were exhibited at the Sprovieri Gallery in April 1914.

49 Balla was much interested in sculptural constructions and made many from impermanent material. One complex relief in the possession of his family was recently refabricated in bronze, but most of the works were lost.

50 The gradual division in Futurist ranks took place throughout 1914. It was signaled by Papini's article, "Il cerchio si chiude," *Lacerba*, II, 4 (15 Feb. 1914), 49–50, and climaxed by "Futurismo e Marinettismo," *Lacerba*, III, 4 (14 February 1915), 49–51, signed by Palazzeschi, Soffici, and Papini and clearly supported by Carrà and probably Severini.

Chronology

NOTE: *This brief chronology is primarily devoted to the activity of the Futurist artists. For a more comprehensive listing see the "Archivi del Futurismo."*

1909

FEBRUARY 20. Marinetti's "Foundation and Manifesto of Futurism," written late in 1908, is published on the front page of *Le Figaro*, Paris. Circulated in Italian first as a broadside, it was again published in both French and Italian in *Poesia*, V, 1–2 (Feb.–Mar. 1909).

FEBRUARY. During the month Marinetti meets Boccioni, Carrà, and Russolo. Shortly thereafter, according to Carrà's recollection, the painters draw up their first manifesto.

APRIL. Marinetti writes "Let's Kill the Moonlight," published in *Poesia*, V, 7–8–9 (Aug.–Sept.–Oct. 1909). Boccioni, Carrà, Russolo, Balla, and Severini are listed among the Futurists.

1910

JANUARY 12. Futurist Manifesto and poetry presented at Politeama Rossetti, Trieste.

FEBRUARY 11. Date assigned to the "Manifesto of Futurist Painters," proclaimed from the stage of the Politeama Chiarella, Turin, March 8. Many manifestoes are dated on the eleventh of the month since Marinetti attached particular importance to that number. Since many of them were published first as broadsides or pamphlets, the dates assigned rarely coincide with those of their first publications in periodicals.

FEBRUARY 15. Futurist reading at the Teatro Lirico, Milan.

MARCH 8. First participation of the artists (Boccioni, Bonzagni, Carrà, Romani, Russolo) in a Futurist presentation, Politeama Chiarella, Turin.

MARCH 19–APRIL 3. Boccioni, Bonzagni, Carrà, and Russolo exhibit prints and drawings at the *Famiglia Artistica* exhibition, Milan. Although the works did not reflect the new ideas, they later referred to this as the first exhibition of Futurist works.

APRIL 11. "Technical Manifesto of Futurist Painting," signed by Balla, Boccioni, Carrà, Russolo, and Severini.

APRIL 20. Boccioni, Carrà, Bonzagni, and Russolo take part in a Futurist presentation at the Teatro Mercadante, Naples.

Sant'Elia, Boccioni, and Marinetti, 1915

JULY 16. Boccioni exhibits forty-two drawings, prints, and paintings at the Ca' Pesaro, Venice. The catalogue presentation by Marinetti describes the Futurist goals.

AUGUST 1. Futurist presentation at La Fenice, Venice. During the day copies of "Futurist Venice," signed by the poets and Boccioni, Bonzagni, Carrà, Russolo, and Severini, are showered from the Torre dell' Orologio.

AUGUST 3. Futurist presentation in Padua.

DECEMBER 20–31. Boccioni, Carrà, and Russolo exhibit in the "Intimate Exhibition" of *Famiglia Artistica*, Milan.

1911

JANUARY 11. "Manifesto of Futurist Music" by Balilla Pratella.

MARCH 25. Futurist presentation in the Teatro Bonacossi, Ferrara.

MARCH 29. "Technical Manifesto of Futurist Music" by Balilla Pratella.

APRIL 6. Futurist presentation at the Teatro Andreini, Mantua.

APRIL 8. Futurist presentation at Parma.

APRIL 21. Futurist presentation at Como.

APRIL 30. Opening of the *Mostra d'Arte Libera*, Padiglione Ricordi, Milan, sponsored by the Casa di Lavoro. Boccioni,

Carrà, and Russolo exhibit many works hung together, widely advertised as Futurist.

MAY 29. Boccioni speaks on Futurism at the *Circolo Artistico Internazionale*, Rome.

JUNE 3. Futurist presentation at the Politeama Garibaldi, Treviso, by Marinetti, Boccioni, Carrà, and Russolo.

JUNE 22. The Futurists assault Soffici and his friends of *La Voce* in Florence for Soffici's adverse criticism of the Futurist paintings in Milan.

OCTOBER–NOVEMBER. Boccioni and Carrà visit Paris briefly with Severini.

1912

FEBRUARY 5–24. Exhibition by the Futurist painters at Bernheim-Jeune, Paris (Boccioni, Carrà, Russolo, and Severini).

MARCH 1. The Futurist exhibition from Paris opens at the Sackville Gallery, London.

APRIL 11. "Manifesto of Futurist Sculpture" by Boccioni.

APRIL 12. The Futurist paintings are shown at the Tiergartenstrasse Gallery, Berlin, as the second exhibition sponsored by Walden and *Der Sturm*. It was immediately preceded by an exhibition of German Expressionist painting. The original Futurist Manifesto (published in *Der Sturm* in March) is used also in a broadside advertising the exhibition. Many of the paintings are sold to Dr. Borchardt for further exhibition.

APRIL (?). Balla paints in Düsseldorf at the home of the lawyer Loewenstein.

MAY 11. "Technical Manifesto of Futurist Literature" by Marinetti, announcing the principle of "Free Words" (*Parole in libertà*). On August 11 he adds a further statement in answer to objections.

JUNE 1. The Futurist exhibition opens at the Salle Giroux, Brussels.

AUGUST. The Futurist paintings at the gallery of J. J. Biesing, The Hague.

SEPTEMBER. The Futurist paintings are shown at the Audretsch Gallery, Amsterdam.

OCTOBER 27. The Futurist exhibition opens at Galerie Thannhauser, Munich.

OCTOBER. Boccioni exhibits some sculpture at the Salon d'Automne, Paris.

1913

JANUARY 1. First issue of *Lacerba*, Florence.

FEBRUARY 21. Tumultuous Futurist presentation at the Teatro Costanzi, Rome. A second presentation at the theater March 9 ends in a riot. An exhibition of Futurist paintings including works by Balla and Soffici is held in the theater from Feb. 21 to March 21.

MARCH 11. "The Art of Noises," manifesto by Russolo addressed to Pratella.

MARCH 18. Apollinaire publishes an article on Delaunay and Orphism in *Montjoie!* that is attacked by Boccioni as plagiarism of Futurist ideas.

APRIL 7. Exhibition of Severini's paintings and drawings opens at the Marlborough Gallery, London. In June the works are exhibited by Walden in Berlin.

MAY 11. Marinetti's manifesto "Wireless Imagination and Free Words."

MAY 18–JUNE 15. Exhibition of Futurist painting and sculpture at Rotterdamsche Kunstkring, Rotterdam.

JUNE 20. Apollinaire's manifesto "Futurist Anti-Tradition." Probably written several months earlier (possibly at the end of 1912), it is published in *Lacerba*, I, 18 (15 Sept. 1913).

JUNE 20–JULY 16. Exhibition of Boccioni's sculpture at the Galerie La Boëtie, Paris. On June 21 Marinetti and on June 27 Boccioni give talks on Futurism in the gallery.

JULY 15. A. F. MacDelmarle's "Futurist Manifesto Against Montmartre" published in *Comoedia*. Severini protests the manifesto in a letter published by the paper July 23.

AUGUST 11. Carrà's manifesto "The Painting of Sounds, Noises, and Smells." Published in *Lacerba*, I, 17 (Sept. 1, 1913).

SEPTEMBER 20. The Futurists exhibit in the *Erster Deutscher Herbstsalon* at Walden's in Berlin.

SEPTEMBER 29. Marinetti's manifesto "The Variety Theater." Published in *Lacerba*, I, 19 (Oct. 1, 1913).

OCTOBER 11. "The Futurist Political Program" signed by Marinetti, Boccioni, Carrà, and Russolo.

NOVEMBER 30–JANUARY 15. Futurist exhibition sponsored by *Lacerba* at the gallery of Ferrante Gonelli, Florence.

DECEMBER 6–JANUARY 15. Boccioni exhibits sculpture and drawings at the Galleria Permanente d'Arte Futurista established in Rome by Giuseppe Sprovieri.

1914

JANUARY 15. Palazzeschi publishes his manifesto, "The Pain Killer," dated Dec. 29, 1913, in *Lacerba*, II, 2 (Jan. 15, 1914).

JANUARY–FEBRUARY. Marinetti lectures to enthusiastic audiences in Moscow and St. Petersburg, meeting the Russian Futurists.

FEBRUARY 11. Exhibition of Futurist works opens at Sprovieri's gallery in Rome.

FEBRUARY 15. Papini's article "The Circle Closes," *Lacerba*, II, 4, marks a split in the Futurist ranks. Boccioni answers with "The Circle Is Not Closing," *Lacerba*, II, 5 (March 1) which is followed by Papini's "Open Circles" in the same issue.

MARCH 15.   Marinetti's manifesto, "Geometric and Mechanical Splendor and the New Numerical Sensibility," is published in *Lacerba*, II, 6. An English translation is published in *The New Age*, London, May 7, 1914.

MARCH.   Boccioni publishes the book *Pittura, Scultura Futuriste*, written in 1913. Carrà takes exception to many passages.

APRIL 13–MAY 25.   First Free International Exhibition of Futurist Art, Sprovieri's gallery, Rome, including the works of many younger painters. Marinetti, Cangiullo, and Balla exhibit their "object sculptures," some of them with joint authorship.

APRIL 21.   Russolo gives an *Intonarumori* concert at the Teatro Dal Verme, Milan.

APRIL 23.   The Futurists participate in the international exhibition of modern art at the Doré Gallery, London. Much publicized are the "object sculptures" by Marinetti and Cangiullo.

MAY 14–JUNE 10.   Futurist exhibition in Naples organized by Giuseppe Sprovieri.

MAY 20–JUNE 10.   First exhibition of the New Tendencies group, including designs by Antonio Sant'Elia, held at the *Famiglia Artistica*, Milan.

JUNE 15.   *Intonarumori* concert at the Coliseum, London.

JULY 11.   Sant'Elia's "Manifesto of Futurist Architecture." Published in *Lacerba*, II, 15 (Aug. 1).

JULY 15.   Marinetti and C. R. W. Nevinson publish the manifesto, "Vital English Art," in Italian and English in *Lacerba*, II, 4.

SEPTEMBER 11.   Balla and Cangiullo's manifesto, "Anti-neutral Clothes."

SEPTEMBER 20.   "The Futurist Synthesis of the War" signed by Boccioni, Carrà, Marinetti, Ercole Piatti, and Russolo. Earlier Marinetti, Boccioni, and Russolo were arrested for staging interventionist demonstrations.

1915

FEBRUARY 1.   "Manifesto of the Futurist Synthetic Theater" by Marinetti, Bruno Corra, and Emilio Settimelli.

FEBRUARY 14.   Papini, Palazzeschi, and Soffici publish "Futurism and Marinettism" in *Lacerba*, marking a decisive split in the Futurist group. Palazzeschi has already published a formal withdrawal from Futurism in *La Voce*, April 28, 1914.

MARCH 11.   Balla and Fortunato Depero sign the manifesto, "The Futurist Reconstruction of the Universe." Balla at this time is experimenting with "plastic complexities," constructions combining various materials.

MAY.   Forty-eight drawings and paintings and Boccioni's sculptures, *Development of a Bottle in Space* and *Muscles in Quick Movement* are shown by the Futurists through the summer at the Panama-Pacific International Exposition, San

Francisco. Boccioni's essay, "The Exhibitors to the Public," is published in the catalogue.

MAY 24.   Italy declares war on Austria.

JULY.   Boccioni, Marinetti, Russolo, Sant'Elia and others join a battalion of volunteer cyclists that goes into action on the front.

DECEMBER 15.   Balla exhibits his work in Rome at a gallery on the Corso.

1916

JANUARY 15–FEBRUARY 1.   Severini holds an exhibition, *Ire Exposition Futuriste d'Art Plastique de la Guerre*, in the Galerie Boutet de Monvel, Paris.

JANUARY 16.   Boccioni, on leave from the army, lectures in Naples on "Plastic Dynamism." On February 28 he lectures at a local exhibition in Mantua.

JUNE.   Boccioni, guest of Ferruccio Busoni, paints the musician's portrait in a style recalling Cézanne. At the end of the month he is recalled to service and assigned to the artillery stationed at Sorte near Verona.

AUGUST 17.   Boccioni dies from injuries sustained the preceding day in a fall from a horse.

SEPTEMBER 11.   Manifesto, "Futurist Cinematography," signed by Marinetti, Balla, Remo Chiti, Bruno Corra, Arnaldo Ginna, and Emilio Settimelli. Arnaldo Ginna makes a short Futurist film, and Anton Giulio Bragalia makes the full length experimental, *Perfido Incanto*.

OCTOBER 10.   Sant'Elia is killed at the front.

DECEMBER 28–JANUARY 14.   Comprehensive exhibition of Boccioni's work at the Galleria Centrale d'Arte, Palazzo Covo, Milan.

Balla in his studio, Rome

Appendix A: Four Futurist Manifestoes

1 INITIAL MANIFESTO OF FUTURISM (February 20, 1909)

2 FUTURIST PAINTING: TECHNICAL MANIFESTO

  (April 11, 1910)

3 THE EXHIBITORS TO THE PUBLIC (February 5, 1912)

4 TECHNICAL MANIFESTO OF FUTURIST SCULPTURE

  (April 11, 1912)

NOTE: The first three manifestoes are here given in the translation published in the catalogue of the exhibition held at the Sackville Gallery, London, in March 1912. These three statements appeared regularly in the exhibition catalogues, and were translated into French and German as well as English. The manifesto on Futurist sculpture was translated recently by Richard Chase.

INITIAL MANIFESTO OF FUTURISM*

(February 20, 1909)

1 We shall sing the love of danger, the habit of energy and boldness.

2 The essential elements of our poetry shall be courage, daring and rebellion.

3 Literature has hitherto glorified thoughtful immobility, ecstasy and sleep; we shall extol aggressive movement, feverish insomnia, the double quick step, the somersault, the box on the ear, the fisticuff.

4 We declare that the world's splendour has been enriched by a new beauty; the beauty of speed. A racing motor-car, its frame adorned with great pipes, like snakes with explosive breath ... a roaring motor-car, which looks as though running on shrapnel, is more beautiful than the *Victory of Samothrace*.

5 We shall sing of the man at the steering wheel, whose ideal stem transfixes the Earth, rushing over the circuit of her orbit.

6 The poet must give himself with frenzy, with splendour and with lavishness, in order to increase the enthusiastic fervour of the primordial elements.

7 There is no more beauty except in strife. No masterpiece without aggressiveness. Poetry must be a violent onslaught upon the unknown forces, to command them to bow before man.

8 We stand upon the extreme promontory of the centuries! ... Why should we look behind us, when we have to break in the mysterious portals of the Impossible? Time and Space died yesterday. Already we live in the absolute, since we have already created speed, eternal and ever-present.

9 We wish to glorify War—the only health giver of the world—militarism, patriotism, the destructive arm of the Anarchist, the beautiful Ideas that kill, the contempt for woman.

10 We wish to destroy the museums, the libraries, to fight against moralism, feminism and all opportunistic and utilitarian meannesses.

11 We shall sing of the great crowds in the excitement of labour, pleasure and rebellion; of the multi-coloured and polyphonic surf of revolutions in modern capital cities; of the nocturnal vibration of arsenals and workshops beneath their violent electric moons; of the greedy stations swallowing smoking snakes; of factories suspended from the clouds by their strings of smoke; of bridges leaping like gymnasts over the diabolical cutlery of sunbathed rivers; of adventurous liners scenting the horizon; of broad-chested locomotives prancing on the rails, like huge steel horses bridled with long tubes; and of the gliding flight of aeroplanes, the sound of whose screw is like the flapping of flags and the applause of an enthusiastic crowd.

It is in Italy that we launch this manifesto of violence, destructive and incendiary, by which we this day found *Futurism*, because we would deliver Italy from its canker of professors, archaeologists, cicerones and antiquaries.

Italy has been too long the great market of the second-hand dealers. We would free her from the numberless museums which cover her with as many cemeteries.

Museums, cemeteries! ... Truly identical with their sinister jostling of bodies that know one another not. Public dormitories where one sleeps for ever side by side with detested or unknown beings. Mutual ferocity of painters and sculptors slaying one another with blows of lines and colour in a single museum.

Let one pay a visit there each year as one visits one's dead once a year ... That we can allow! ... Deposit flowers even once a year at the feet of the *Gioconda*, if you will! ... But to walk daily in the museums with our sorrows, our fragile courage and our anxiety, that is inadmissible! ... Would you, then, poison yourselves? Do you want to decay?

* First published in *Le Figaro*, Paris.

What can one find in an old picture unless it be the painful contortions of the artist striving to break the bars that stand in the way of his desire to express completely his dream?

To admire an old picture is to pour our sensitiveness into a funeral urn, instead of casting it forward in violent gushes of creation and action. Would you, then, waste the best of your strength by a useless administration of the past, from which you can but emerge exhausted, reduced, downtrodden?

In truth, the daily haunting of museums, of libraries and of academies (those cemeteries of wasted efforts, those calvaries of crucified dreams, those ledgers of broken attempts!) is to artists what the protracted tutelage of parents is to intelligent youths, intoxicated with their talent and their ambitious determination.

For men on their death-bed, for invalids, and for prisoners, very well! The admirable past may be balsam to their wounds, since the future is closed to them ... But we will have none of it, we, the young, the strong, and the living *Futurists!*

Come, then, the good incendiaries, with their charred fingers! ... Here they come! Here they come! ... Set fire to the shelves of the libraries! Deviate the course of canals to flood the cellars of the museums! Oh! may the glorious canvases drift helplessly! Seize pickaxes and hammers! Sap the foundations of the venerable cities!

The oldest amongst us are thirty; we have, therefore, ten years at least to accomplish our task. When we are forty, let others, younger and more valiant, throw us into the basket like useless manuscripts! ... They will come against us from afar, from everywhere, bounding upon the lightsome measure of their first poems, scratching the air with their hooked fingers, and scenting at the academy doors the pleasant odour of our rotting minds, marked out already for the catacombs of the libraries.

But we shall not be there. They will find us at length, one winter's night, right out in the country, beneath a dreary shed, the monotonous rain-drops strumming on the roof, cowering by our trepidating aeroplanes, warming our hands at the miserable fire which our books of today will make, blazing gaily beneath the dazzling flight of their images.

They will surge around us, breathless with anxiety and disappointment, and all, exasperated by our dauntless courage, will throw themselves upon us to slay us, with all the more hatred because their hearts will be filled with love and admiration for us. And Injustice, strong and healthy, will burst forth radiantly in their eyes. For art can be nought but violence, cruelty and injustice.

The oldest amongst us are thirty, and yet we have already squandered treasures, treasures of strength, of love, of courage, of rugged determination, hastily, in a frenzy, without counting, with all our might, breathlessly.

Look at us! We are not breathless ... Our heart does not feel the slightest weariness! For it is fed with fire, hatred and speed! ... That surprises you? It is because you do not remember even having lived! We stand upon the summit of the world and once more we cast our challenge to the stars!

Your objections? Enough! Enough! I know them! It is agreed! We know well what our fine and false intelligence tells us. We are, it says, only the summary and the extension of our ancestors. Perhaps! Very well! ... What matter? ... But we do not wish to hear! Beware of repeating those infamous words! Better lift your head!

We stand upon the summit of the world and once more we cast our challenge to the stars!

F. T. Marinetti

Editor of *Poesia*

FUTURIST PAINTING:

TECHNICAL MANIFESTO *(April 11, 1910)*

On the 8th of March, 1910, in the limelight of the Chiarella Theatre of Turin, we launched our first Manifesto to a public of three thousand people—artists, men of letters, students and others; it was a violent and cynical cry which displayed our sense of rebellion, our deep-rooted disgust, our haughty contempt for vulgarity, for academic and pedantic mediocrity, for the fanatical worship of all that is old and worm-eaten.

We bound ourselves there and then to the movement of Futurist Poetry which was initiated a year earlier by F. T. Marinetti in the columns of the *Figaro*.

The battle of Turin has remained legendary. We exchanged almost as many knocks as we did ideas, in order to protect from certain death the genius of Italian Art.

And now during a temporary pause in this formidable struggle we come out of the crowd in order to expound with technical precision our programme for the renovation of painting, of which our Futurist Salon at Milan was a dazzling manifestation.*

Our growing need of truth is no longer satisfied with Form and Colour as they have been understood hitherto.

The gesture which we would reproduce on canvas shall no longer be a fixed *moment* in universal dynamism. It shall simply be the dynamic sensation itself [made eternal].

Indeed, all things move, all things run, all things are rapidly changing.

A profile is never motionless before our eyes, but it constantly appears and disappears. On account of the persistency of an image upon the retina, moving objects constantly multiply themselves; their form changes like rapid vibrations, in their mad career. Thus a running horse has not four legs, but twenty, and their movements are triangular.

All is conventional in art. Nothing is absolute in painting. What was truth for the painters of yesterday is but a falsehood to-day. We declare, for instance, that a portrait [to be a work of art] must not be like the sitter and that the painter

* The "Salon" referred to is the "Mostra d'arte libera," opened April 30, 1911. In most versions of the manifesto the following significant paragraph took the place of the above: "We were concerned then with relation between ourselves and society. Today, instead, with this second manifesto, we resolutely shake off all relative considerations and ascend to the highest expressions of the pictorial absolute."

carries in himself the landscapes which he would fix upon his canvas.

To paint a human figure you must not paint it; you must render the whole of its surrounding atmosphere.

Space no longer exists: The street pavement, soaked by rain beneath the glare of electric lamps, becomes immensely deep and gapes to the very centre of the earth. Thousands of miles divide us from the sun; yet the house in front of us fits into the solar disk.

Who can still believe in the opacity of bodies, since our sharpened and multiplied sensitiveness has already penetrated the obscure manifestations of the medium? Why should we forget in our creations the doubled power of our sight, capable of giving results analogous to those of the X rays?

It will be sufficient to cite a few examples, chosen amongst thousands, to prove the truth of our arguments.

The sixteen people around you in a rolling motor-bus are in turn and at the same time one, ten, four, three; they are motionless and they change places; they come and go, bound into the street, are suddenly swallowed up by the sunshine, then come back and sit before you, like persistent symbols of universal vibration.

How often have we not seen upon the cheek of the person with whom we were talking the horse which passes at the end of the street.

Our bodies penetrate the sofas upon which we sit, and the sofas penetrate our bodies. The motor-bus rushes into the houses which it passes, and in their turn the houses throw themselves upon the motor-bus and are blended with it.

The construction of pictures has hitherto been foolishly traditional. Painters have shown us the objects and the people placed before us. We shall henceforward put the spectator in the centre of the picture.

As in every realm of the human mind, clear-sighted individual research has swept away the unchanging obscurities of dogma, so must the vivifying current of science soon deliver painting from academic tradition.

We would at any price re-enter into life. Victorious science has nowadays disowned its past in order the better to serve the material needs of our time; we would that art, disowning its past, were able to serve at last the intellectual needs which are within us.

Our renovated consciousness does not permit us to look upon man as the centre of universal life. The suffering of a man is of the same interest to us as the suffering of an electric lamp, which, with spasmodic starts, shrieks out the most heartrending expressions of colour.** The harmony of the lines and folds of modern dress works upon our sensitiveness with the same emotional and symbolical power as did the nude upon the sensitiveness of the old masters.

In order to conceive and understand the novel beauties of a futurist picture, the soul must be purified [become again pure]; the eye must be freed from its veil of atavism and culture, so that it may at last look upon Nature and not upon the museum as the one and only standard.

As soon as ever this result has been obtained, it will be readily admitted that brown tints have never coursed beneath our skin; it will be discovered that yellow shines forth in our flesh, that red blazes, and that green, blue and violet dance upon it with untold charms, voluptuous and caressing.

How is it possible still to see the human face pink, now that our life, redoubled by noctambulism, has multiplied our perceptions as colourists? The human face is yellow, red, green, blue, violet. The palor of a woman gazing in a jeweller's window is more intensely iridescent than the prismatic fires of the jewels that fascinate her like a lark.

The time has passed for our sensations in painting to be whispered. We wish them in future to sing and re-echo upon our canvases in deafening and triumphant flourishes.

Your eyes, accustomed to semi-darkness, will soon open to more radiant visions of light. The shadows which we shall paint shall be more luminous than the high-lights of our predecessors, and our pictures, next to those of the museums, will shine like blinding daylight compared with deepest night.

We conclude that painting cannot exist to-day without Divisionism. This is no process that can be learned and applied at will. Divisionism, for the modern painter, must be an INNATE COMPLEMENTARINESS which we declare to be essential and necessary.

Our art will probably be accused of tormented and decadent cerebralism. But we shall merely answer that we are, on the contrary, the primitives of a new sensitiveness, multiplied hundredfold, and that our art is intoxicated with spontaneity and power.†

WE DECLARE:

1 THAT ALL FORMS OF IMITATION MUST BE DESPISED, ALL FORMS OF ORIGINALITY GLORIFIED.

2 THAT IT IS ESSENTIAL TO REBEL AGAINST THE TYRANNY OF THE TERMS "HARMONY" AND "GOOD TASTE" AS BEING TOO ELASTIC EXPRESSIONS, BY THE HELP OF WHICH IT IS EASY TO DEMOLISH THE WORKS OF REMBRANDT, OF GOYA AND OF RODIN.

3 THAT THE ART CRITICS ARE USELESS OR HARMFUL.

4 THAT ALL SUBJECTS PREVIOUSLY USED MUST BE SWEPT ASIDE IN ORDER TO EXPRESS OUR WHIRLING LIFE OF STEEL, OF PRIDE, OF FEVER AND OF SPEED.

5 THAT THE NAME OF "MADMAN" WITH WHICH IT IS ATTEMPTED TO GAG ALL INNOVATORS SHOULD BE LOOKED UPON AS A TITLE OF HONOUR.

---

† In the publication of the collected manifestoes, in 1914, the following takes the place of this paragraph: "Finally, we reject the easy accusation of 'baroquism' with which some would like to confront us. The ideas we have presented here derive solely from our acute sensibility. While 'baroquism' signifies artificiality irresponsible and devitalized virtuosity, the art we set forth is all spontaneity and power."

** In other publications this reads "expressions of grief."

6 THAT INNATE COMPLEMENTARINESS IS AN ABSOLUTE NECESSITY IN PAINTING, JUST AS FREE METRE IN POETRY OR POLYPHONY IN MUSIC.

7 THAT UNIVERSAL DYNAMISM MUST BE RENDERED IN PAINTING AS A DYNAMIC SENSATION.

8 THAT IN THE MANNER OF RENDERING NATURE THE FIRST ESSENTIAL IS IN SINCERITY AND PURITY.

9 THAT MOVEMENT AND LIGHT DESTROY THE MATERIALITY OF BODIES.

WE FIGHT:

1 AGAINST THE BITUMINOUS TINTS BY WHICH IT IS ATTEMPTED TO OBTAIN THE PATINA OF TIME UPON MODERN PICTURES.

2 AGAINST THE SUPERFICIAL AND ELEMENTARY ARCHAISM FOUNDED UPON FLAT TINTS, AND WHICH, BY IMITATING THE LINEAR TECHNIQUE OF THE EGYPTIANS, REDUCES PAINTING TO A POWERLESS SYNTHESIS, BOTH CHILDISH AND GROTESQUE.

3 AGAINST THE FALSE CLAIMS TO BELONG TO THE FUTURE PUT FORWARD BY THE SECESSIONISTS AND THE INDEPENDENTS, WHO HAVE INSTALLED NEW ACADEMIES NO LESS TRITE AND ATTACHED TO ROUTINE THAN THE PRECEDING ONES.

4 AGAINST THE NUDE IN PAINTING, AS NAUSEOUS AND AS TEDIOUS AS ADULTERY IN LITERATURE.

We wish to explain this last point. Nothing is *immoral* in our eyes; it is the monotony of the nude against which we fight. We are told that the subject is nothing and that everything lies in the manner of treating it. That is agreed; we, too, admit that. But this truism, unimpeachable and absolute fifty years ago, is no longer so to-day with regard to the nude, since artists obsessed with the desire to expose the bodies of their mistresses have transformed the Salons into arrays of unwholesome flesh!

We demand, for ten years, the total suppression of the nude in painting.††

UMBERTO BOCCIONI, *painter* (Milan).

CARLO D. CARRÀ, *painter* (Milan).

LUIGI RUSSOLO, *painter* (Milan).

GIACOMO BALLA, *painter* (Rome).

GINO SEVERINI, *painter* (Paris).

†† In the publication of the collected manifestoes in 1914 these final two paragraphs were omitted. In their place was the following:

"You think us mad. We are, instead, the primitives of a new, completely transformed, sensibility."

"Outside the atmosphere in which we live are only shadows. We futurists ascend towards the highest and most radiant peak and proclaim ourselves Lords of Light, for already we drink from the live founts of the sun."

---

*THE EXHIBITORS TO THE PUBLIC**

(*February 5, 1912*)

We may declare, without boasting, that the first Exhibition of Italian Futurist Painting, recently held in Paris and now brought to London, is the most important exhibition of Italian painting which has hitherto been offered to the judgment of Europe.

For we are young and our art is violently revolutionary.

What we have attempted and accomplished, while attracting around us a large number of skilful imitators and as many plagiarists without talent, has placed us at the head of the European movement in painting, by a road different from, yet, in a way, parallel with that followed by the Post-impressionists, Synthetists, and Cubists of France, led by their masters Picasso, Braque, Derain, Metzinger, Le Fauconnier, Gleizes, Léger, Lhote, etc.

While we admire the heroism of these painters of great worth, who have displayed a laudable contempt for artistic commercialism and a powerful hatred of academism, we feel ourselves and we declare ourselves to be absolutely opposed to their art.

They obstinately continue to paint objects motionless, frozen, and all the static aspects of Nature; they worship the traditionalism of Poussin, of Ingres, of Corot, aging and petrifying their art with an obstinate attachment to the past, which to our eyes remains totally incomprehensible.

We, on the contrary, with points of view pertaining essentially to the future, seek for a style of motion, a thing which has never been attempted before us.

Far from resting upon the examples of the Greeks and the Old Masters, we constantly extol individual intuition; our object is to determine completely new laws which may deliver painting from the wavering uncertainly in which it lingers.

Our desire, to give as far as possible to our pictures a solid construction, can never bear us back to any tradition whatsoever. Of that we are firmly convinced.

All the truths learnt in the schools or in the studios are abolished for us. Our hands are free enough and pure enough to start everything afresh.

It is indisputable that several of the aesthetic declarations of our French comrades display a sort of masked academism.

Is it not, indeed, a return to the Academy to declare that the subject, in painting, is of perfectly insignificant value?

We declare, on the contrary, that there can be no modern painting without the starting point of an absolutely modern sensation, and none can contradict us when we state that *painting* and *sensation* are two inseparable words.

If our pictures are futurist, it is because they are the result of absolutely futurist conceptions, ethical, aesthetic, political and social.

To paint from the posing model is an absurdity, and an act of mental cowardice, even if the model be translated upon the picture in linear, spherical or cubic forms.

* First published (in French) for the exhibition at Bernheim-Jeune, Paris, February 5–12, 1912.

To lend an allegorical significance to an ordinary nude figure, deriving the meaning of the picture from the objects held by the model or from those which are arranged about him, is to our mind the evidence of a traditional and academic mentality.

This method, very similar to that employed by the Greeks, by Raphael, by Titian, by Veronese, must necessarily displease us.

While we repudiate impressionism, we emphatically condemn the present reaction which, in order to kill impressionism, brings back painting to old academic forms.

It is only possible to react against impressionism by surpassing it.

Nothing is more absurd than to fight it by adopting the pictural laws which preceded it.

The points of contact which the quest of style may have with the so-called *classic art* do not concern us.

Others will seek, and will, no doubt, discover, these analogies which in any case cannot be looked upon as a return to methods, conceptions and values transmitted by classical painting.

A few examples will illustrate our theory.

We see no difference between one of those nude figures commonly called *artistic* and an anatomical plate. There is, on the other hand, an enormous difference between one of these nude figures and our futurist conception of the human body.

Perspective, such as it is understood by the majority of painters, has for us the very same value which they give to an engineer's design.

The simultaneousness of states of mind in the work of art: that is the intoxicating aim of our art.

Let us explain again by examples. In painting a person on a balcony, seen from inside the room, we do not limit the scene to what the square frame of the window renders visible; but we try to render the sum total of visual sensations which the person on the balcony has experienced; the sun-bathed throng in the street, the double row of houses which stretch to right and left, the beflowered balconies, etc. This implies the simultaneousness of the ambient, and, therefore, the dislocation and dismemberment of objects, the scattering and fusion of details, freed from accepted logic, and independent from one another.*

In order to make the spectator live in the centre of the picture, as we express it in our manifesto, the picture must be the synthesis of *what one remembers and of what one sees.*

You must render the invisible which stirs and lives beyond intervening obstacles, what we have on the right, on the left, and behind us, and not merely the small square of life artificially compressed, as it were, by the wings of a stage.

We have declared in our manifesto that what must be rendered is the *dynamic sensation*, that is to say, the particu-

lar rhythm of each object, its inclination, its movement, or, to put it more exactly, its interior force.

It is usual to consider the human being in its different aspects of motion or stillness, of joyous excitement or grave melancholy.

What is overlooked is that all inanimate objects display, by their lines, calmness or frenzy, sadness or gaiety. These various tendencies lend to the lines of which they are formed a sense and character of weighty stability or of aerial lightness.

Every object reveals by its lines how it would resolve itself were it to follow the tendencies of its forces.

This decomposition is not governed by fixed laws but it varies according to the characteristic personality of the object and the emotions of the onlooker.

Furthermore, every object influences its neighbour, not by reflections of light (the foundation of *impressionistic primitivism*), but by a real competition of lines and by real conflicts of planes, following the emotional law which governs the picture (the foundation of *futurist primitivism*).

With the desire to intensify the aesthetic emotions by blending, so to speak, the painted canvas with the soul of the spectator, we have declared that the latter "*must in future be placed in the centre of the picture.*"

He shall not be present at, but participate in the action. If we paint the phases of a riot, the crowd bustling with uplifted fists and the noisy onslaughts of cavalry are translated upon the canvas in sheaves of lines corresponding with all the conflicting forces, following the general law of violence of the picture.

These *force-lines* must encircle and involve the spectator so that he will in a manner be forced to struggle himself with the persons in the picture.

All objects, in accordance with what the painter Boccioni happily terms *physical transcendentalism*, tend to the infinite by their *force-lines* the continuity of which is measured by our intuition.

It is these *force-lines* that we must draw in order to lead back the work of art to true painting. We interpret nature by rendering these objects upon the canvas as the beginnings or the prolongations of the rhythms impressed upon our sensibility by these very objects.

After having, for instance, reproduced in a picture the right shoulder or the right ear of a figure, we deem it totally vain and useless to reproduce the left shoulder or the left ear. We do not draw sounds, but their vibrating intervals. We do not paint diseases, but their symptoms and the consequences.

We may further explain our idea by a comparison drawn from the evolution of music.

Not only have we radically abandoned the motive fully developed according to its determined and, therefore, artificial equilibrium, but we suddenly and purposely intersect each motive with one or more other motives of which we never give the full development but merely the initial, central, or final notes.

As you see, there is with us not merely variety, but chaos and clashing of rhythms, totally opposed to one another, which we nevertheless assemble into a new harmony.

---

* Boccioni, who was chiefly responsible for this preface, here describes his *The Noise of the Street Penetrates the House.*

We thus arrive at what we call the *painting of states of mind.*

In the pictorial description of the various states of mind of a leave-taking, perpendicular lines, undulating and as it were worn out, cling here and there to silhouettes of empty bodies, may well express languidness and discouragement.

Confused and trepidating lines, either straight or curved, mingled with the outlined hurried gestures of people calling one another, will express a sensation of chaotic excitement.

On the other hand, horizontal lines, fleeting, rapid and jerky, brutally cutting into half lost profiles of faces or crumbling and rebounding fragments of landscape, will give the tumultuous feelings of the persons going away.

It is practically impossible to express in words the essential values of painting.

The public must also be convinced that in order to understand aesthetic sensations to which one is not accustomed, it is necessary to forget entirely one's intellectual culture, not in order to *assimilate* the work of art, but to *deliver one's self up* to it heart and soul.

We are beginning a new epoch of painting.

We are sure henceforward of realizing conceptions of the highest importance and the most unquestionable originality. Others will follow who, with equal daring and determination will conquer those summits of which we can only catch a glimpse. That is why we have proclaimed ourselves to be *the primitives of a completely renovated sensitiveness.*

In several of the pictures which we are presenting to the public, vibration and motion endlessly multiply each object. We have thus justified our famous statement regarding the *"running horse which has not four legs, but twenty."*

One may remark, also, in our pictures spots, lines, zones of colour which do not correspond to any reality, but which, in accordance with a law of our interior mathematics, musically prepare and enhance the emotion of the spectator.

We thus create a sort of emotive ambience, seeking by intuition the sympathies and the links which exist between the exterior (concrete) scene and the interior (abstract) emotion. Those lines, those spots, those zones of colour, apparently illogical and meaningless, are the mysterious keys to our pictures.

We shall no doubt be taxed with an excessive desire to define and express in tangible form the subtle ties which unite our abstract interior with the concrete exterior.

Yet, could we leave an unfettered liberty of understanding to the public which always sees as it has been taught to see, through eyes warped by routine?

We go our way, destroying each day in ourselves and in our pictures the realistic forms and the obvious details which have served us to construct a bridge of understanding between ourselves and the public. In order that the crowd may enjoy our marvellous spiritual world, of which it is ignorant, we give it the material sensation of that world.

We thus reply to the coarse and simplistic curiosity which surrounds us by the brutally realistic aspects of our primitivism.

Conclusion: Our futurist painting embodies three new conceptions of painting:

1 That which solves the question of volumes in a picture, as opposed to the liquefaction of objects favoured by the vision of the impressionists.

2 That which leads us to translate objects according to the *force-lines* which distinguish them, and by which is obtained an absolutely new power of objective poetry.

3 That (the natural consequence of the other two) which would give the emotional ambience of a picture, the synthesis of the various abstract rhythms of every object, from which there springs a fount of pictural lyricism hitherto unknown.

UMBERTO BOCCIONI

CARLO D. CARRÀ

LUIGI RUSSOLO

GIACOMO BALLA

GINO SEVERINI

N.B. All the ideas contained in this preface were developed at length in the lecture on Futurist Painting, delivered by the painter, Boccioni, at the Circolo Internazionale Artistico, at Rome, on May 29th, 1911.

ESSENTIAL TO FUTURIST AESTHETIC: RECOGNIZE CHANGING VALUES IN ART.

TECHNICAL MANIFESTO OF FUTURIST SCULPTURE

Umberto Boccioni   (April 11, 1912)

In the monuments and exhibitions of every European city, sculpture offers a spectacle of such pitiable barbarism, clumsiness, and monotonous imitation, that my Futurist eye recoils from it with profound disgust!

The sculpture of every country is dominated by the blind and foolish imitation of formulas inherited from the past, an imitation encouraged by the double cowardice of tradition and facility. In Latin countries we have the burdensome weight of Greece and Michelangelo which is borne in France and Belgium with a certain seriousness of skill, and in Italy with grotesque imbecility. In German countries we have a foolish Greek-ized Gothicism, industrialized in Berlin, and in Munich sweetened with effeminate care by German pedantry. In Slavic countries, on the other hand, there is a confused clash between archaic Greek and Nordic and Oriental monstrosities, a shapeless mass of influences that range from the excess of abstruse details deriving from Asia, to the childish and grotesque ingenuity of the Lapps and Eskimos.

In all these manifestations of sculpture, as well as in those with a larger measure of innovating audacity, the same error is perpetuated: the artist copies the nude and studies classical statuary with the simple minded conviction that he can find a style corresponding to modern sensibility without relinquishing the traditional concept of sculptural form. This concept, with its famous "ideal beauty" of which everyone speaks on bended knee, never breaks away from the Phidian period and its decadence.

And it is almost inexplicable why the thousands of sculptors who have continued from generation to generation to construct dummies have not as yet asked themselves why the galleries of sculpture, when not absolutely deserted, are visited with boredom and horror, and why the unveiling of monuments in squares all over the world meets with incomprehension and general hilarity. This does not happen with painting because of its continual renewal which, as slow as the process has been, is the clearest condemnation of the plagiarized and sterile works of all the sculptors of our epoch!

Sculptors must convince themselves of this absolute truth: to continue to construct and want to create with Egyptian, Greek, or Michelangelesque elements, is like wanting to draw water from a dry well with a bottomless bucket.

There can be no renewal in art whatever if the essence itself is not renewed, that is, the vision and concept of line and masses that form the arabesque. It is not simply by reproducing the exterior aspects of contemporary life that art becomes the expression of its own time; this is why sculpture as it has been understood to date by artists of the past century and the present is a monstrous anachronism!

Sculpture has failed to progress because of the limited field assigned to it by the academic concept of the nude. An art that has to completely strip a man or woman in order to begin its emotive function is a dead art! Painting has taken on new life, profundity, and breadth through a study of landscape and the environment, which are made to react simultaneously in relationship to the human figures or objects, reaching the point of our Futurist INTERPENETRATION OF PLANES (*Technical Manifesto of Futurist Painting*, April 11, 1910). In the same way sculpture will find a new source of emotion, hence of style, extending its plastic quality to what our barbarous crudity has made us think of until now as subdivided, impalpable, and thus plastically inexpressible.

We have to start from the central nucleus of the object that we want to create, in order to discover the new laws, that is, the new forms, that link it invisibly but mathematically to the APPARENT PLASTIC INFINITE and to the INTERNAL PLASTIC INFINITE. The new plastic art will, then, be a translation into plaster, bronze, glass, wood, and any other material, of those atmospheric planes that link and intersect things. This vision that I have called PHYSICAL TRANSCENDENTALISM (*Lecture on Futurist Painting at the Circolo Artistico*, Rome, May 1911) will be able to give plastic form to the mysterious sympathies and affinities that the reciprocal formal influences of the planes of objects create.

Sculpture must, therefore, give life to objects by making their extension in space palpable, systematic, and plastic, since no one can any longer believe that an object ends where another begins and that our body is surrounded by anything —bottle, automobile, house, tree, road—that does not cut through it and section it in an arabesque of directional curves.

There have been two attempts at renewal in modern sculpture: one decorative concentrating on style; and the other strictly plastic concentrating on material. The first, anonymous and disordered, lacked a coordinating technical genius and, since it was too closely tied to the economic requirements of building, only produced pieces of traditional sculpture more or less decoratively synthesized and confined within architectural or decorative motives or schemes. All the buildings and houses constructed in accordance with modern criteria include such efforts in marble, cement, or in metal plate.

The second attempt, more pleasing, disinterested, and poetic, but too isolated and fragmentary, lacked a synthetic idea to give it law. In working towards renewal it is not enough just to believe with fervor; one must formulate and work out a norm that points the way. I am referring to the genius of Medardo Rosso, to an Italian, and to the only great modern sculptor who has attempted to open up a larger field to sculpture, rendering plastically the influences of an ambiance and the atmospheric ties that bind it to the subject.

Of the three other great contemporary sculptors, Constantin Meunier has contributed nothing new to sculptural sensibility. His statues are almost always agreeable fusions of the Greek heroic with the athletic humility of the stevedore, sailor, or miner. His plastic and constructional concept of the statue and of bas-relief is still that of the Parthenon or the classical hero, although it was he who first attempted to create and deify subjects that had been previously despised or relegated to lower types of realistic reproduction.

Bourdelle brings to the sculptural block an almost fanatic severity of abstract architectural masses. Of passionate temperament, highly strung, sincerely looking for the truth, he none the less does not know how to free himself from a certain archaic influence and from the general anonymity of the stonecutters of the Gothic cathedrals.

Rodin is of vaster spiritual agility, which has allowed him to go from the Impressionism of the *Balzac* to the uncertainty of the *Burghers of Calais* and all the other Michelangelesque sins. He bears in his sculpture a restless inspiration and a sweeping lyrical drive, which would be truly modern if Michelangelo and Donatello had not already possessed these qualities in almost identical form four hundred or so years before, and if they were used to animate a completely recreated reality.

We thus have in the works of these three great sculptors influences coming from three different periods: Greek in Meunier, Gothic in Bourdelle, Italian Renaissance in Rodin.

The work of Medardo Rosso, on the other hand, is very modern and revolutionary, more profound and of necessity restricted. It involves neither heroes nor symbols, but the plane of a woman's brow, or of a child's, points towards a liberation of space, which will have a much greater importance in the history of the spirit than our times have given it. Unfortunately the impressionistic necessities of this attempt have limited Medardo Rosso's research to a kind of high or low relief, demonstrating that the human figure is still conceived of as a world in itself with traditional bases and an episodic goal.

The revolution of Medardo Rosso, although of the greatest

importance, starts off from an external pictorial concept that overlooks the problem of a new construction of planes; while the sensual touch of the thumb, imitating the lightness of Impressionist brushstrokes, gives a sense of lively immediacy, it requires rapid execution from life and removes from the work of art its character of universal creation. It thus has the same strong points and defects as Impressionism in painting. Our aesthetic revolution also takes its start from these researches, but in continuing them it has gone on to reach an extreme opposite point.

In sculpture as in painting one cannot renovate without searching for THE STYLE OF THE MOVEMENT, that is, by making systematic and definitive in a synthesis what Impressionism has given us as fragmentary, accidental, and thus analytical. And this systematization of the vibrations of light and the interpenetration of planes will produce Futurist sculpture, whose foundation will be architectural, not only in the construction of the masses, but in such a way that the block of the sculpture will contain within itself the architectural elements of the SCULPTURAL ENVIRONMENT in which the subject lives.

Naturally we will bring forth a SCULPTURE OF ENVIRONMENT.

A Futurist composition in sculpture will embody the marvelous mathematical and geometrical elements that make up the objects of our time. And these objects will not be placed next to the statue as explanatory attributes or dislocated decorative elements but, following the laws of a new conception of harmony, will be imbedded in the muscular lines of the body. Thus from the shoulder of a mechanic may protrude the wheel of a machine, and the line of a table might cut into the head of a person reading; and a book with its fan-like leaves might intersect the stomach of the reader.

Traditionally a statue is carved out or delineated against the atmospheric environment in which it is exhibited. Futurist painting has overcome this conception of the rhythmic continuity of the lines in a human figure and of the figure's isolation from its background and from its INVISIBLE INVOLVING SPACE. Futurist poetry, according to the poet Marinetti, "after having destroyed the traditional meter and created free verse, now destroys syntax and the Latin sentence. Futurist poetry is an uninterrupted and spontaneous flow of analogies, each one of which is intuitively related to the central subject. Thus, wireless imagination and free words." The Futurist music of Balilla Pratella breaks through the chronometrical tyranny of rhythm.

Why should sculpture remain behind, tied to laws that no one has the right to impose on it? We therefore cast all aside and proclaim the ABSOLUTE AND COMPLETE ABOLITION OF DEFINITE LINES AND CLOSED SCULPTURE. WE BREAK OPEN THE FIGURE AND ENCLOSE IT IN ENVIRONMENT. We proclaim that the environment must be part of the plastic block which is a world in itself with its own laws; that the sidewalk can jump up on your table and your head be transported across the street, while your lamp spins a web of plaster rays between one house and another.

We proclaim that the whole visible world must fall in upon us, merging with us and creating a harmony measurable only by the creative imagination; that a leg, an arm, or an object, having no importance except as elements of plastic rhythm, can be abolished, not in order to imitate a Greek or Roman fragment, but to conform to the harmony the artist wishes to create. A sculptural entity, like a picture, can only resemble itself, for in art the human figure and objects must exist apart from the logic of physiognomy.

Thus a human figure may have one arm clothed and the other bare, and the different lines of a vase of flowers might freely intervene between the lines of the hat and those of the neck.

Thus transparent planes, glass, sheets of metal, wires, outside or inside electric lights can indicate the planes, inclinations, tones, and half-tones of a new reality.

Thus a new intuitive coloring in white, in gray, in black, can increase the emotive strength of planes, while the note of a colored plane will accentuate with violence the abstract significance of the plastic reality!

What we have said about LINES/FORCES in painting (*Preface-Manifesto of the Catalogue of the First Futurist Exhibition*, Paris, October 1911*) can be said similarly of sculpture; the static muscular line can be made to live in the dynamic line/force. The straight line will predominate in this muscular line, since only it corresponds to the internal simplicity of the synthesis that we oppose to the external baroquism deriving from analysis.

But the straight line will not lead us to imitate the Egyptians, the primitives, and the savages as some modern sculptors have desperately attempted to do in order to free themselves from the Greeks. Our straight line is alive and palpitating; it will lend itself to all that is necessary for the infinite expressions of the material; and its bare, fundamental severity will symbolize the severity of steel that determines the lines of modern machinery.

Finally we can affirm that in sculpture the artist must not shrink from using any means that will allow him to achieve REALITY. There is no fear more stupid than that which makes us afraid to go beyond the bounds of the art we are practicing. There is no such thing as painting, sculpture, music, or poetry; there is only creation! Therefore if a composition is in need of a special rhythmical movement to aid or contrast with the static rhythm of the SCULPTURAL ENTITY (a necessity in a work of art), one can superimpose any structure whatsoever that is capable of giving the required movements to the planes or lines.

We cannot forget that the tick-tock and the moving hands of a clock, the in-and-out of a piston in a cylinder, the opening and closing of two cogwheels with the continual appearance and disappearance of their square steel cogs, the fury of a flywheel or the turbine of a propeller, are all plastic and pictorial elements of which a Futurist work in sculpture

* The exhibition was held in February 1912, although Boccioni noted he had earlier expounded on the ideas included in the preface to the catalogue.

must take account. The opening and closing of a valve creates a rhythm just as beautiful but infinitely newer than the blinking of an animal eyelid.

CONCLUSIONS

1 We proclaim that sculpture is based on the abstract reconstruction of the planes and volumes that determine the forms, not their figurative value.

2 ABOLISH IN SCULPTURE as in every other art THE TRADITIONAL SUBLIMITY OF THE SUBJECT.

3 Deny to sculpture as an aim any "true-to-life" episodic construction, but affirm the absolute necessity of using all reality in order to return to the essential elements of plastic sensibility. Thus, in perceiving bodies and their parts as PLASTIC ZONES, a Futurist composition in sculpture will use metal or wood planes for an object, static or moved mechanically, furry spherical forms for hair, semicircles of glass for a vase, wire and screen for an atmospheric plane, etc.

4 Destroy the wholly literary and traditional nobility of marble and of bronze. Deny the exclusiveness of one material for the entire construction of a sculptural ensemble. Affirm that even twenty different materials can compete in a single work to effect plastic emotion. Let us enumerate some: glass, wood, cardboard, iron, cement, horsehair, leather, cloth, mirrors, electric lights, etc., etc.

5 Proclaim that in the intersection of the planes of a book with the angles of a table, in the lines of a match, in the frame of a window, there is more truth than in all the twisting of muscles, all the breasts and buttocks of the heroes and Venuses that inspire the modern idiocy in sculpture.

6 That only the most modern choice of subjects can lead to the discovery of new PLASTIC IDEAS.

7 That the straight line is the only means that can lead to the primitive virginity of a new architectural construction of sculptural masses or zones.

8 That there can be no renovation if not through a SCULPTURE OF ENVIRONMENT, for through this plasticity will be developed and, continuing, will be able to MODEL THE ATMOSPHERE that surrounds things.

9 The thing that one creates is nothing other than a bridge between the EXTERIOR PLASTIC INFINITE and the INTERIOR PLASTIC INFINITE; thus objects never end, and intersect with infinite combinations of sympathetic harmonies and clashing aversions.

Appendix B: Boccioni Letters to Vico Baer

Translated by Margaret Scolari Barr

Savoy Hotel, London

March 10, 1912

I have not written you before because, in Paris, I kept waiting for a telegram that would announce your arrival ... now the exhibition is closed and I am already in London. In an hour the opening will take place for the press, tomorrow for the public. Journalists already began to come in yesterday, and I foresee that in London too the exhibition will arouse enormous interest.

Do you know that we came here with a magnificent contract?

After London we are practically signed with an important German house in Berlin that is bombarding us with favorable suggestions. Good proposals reach us also from The Hague, Brussels, Dublin, Liège, and Amsterdam.

The Paris show has acquainted all Europe with a new movement that is formidably enthusiastic and robustly youthful. My preface to the catalogue awakened so much interest and acclaim that 17,000 copies were printed; even now with the show closed they are still selling. The English catalogue is good too. The dealer saw fit to add explanations of every single painting—I'm sure they are curious—but they'll be useful for these *bestie di inglesi*—these English blockheads as Benvenuto Cellini once said. Let's face it, the public is imbecile in every country and just as it does not understand in Italy, it does not understand here [in England] and it does not understand in France. In France, however, there is a greater interest in contemporary intellectual matters, art circles are more numerous and the ambition to be an innovator, the leader of a movement with no eye on immediate success is better understood. But in Italy I am considered a talent that is going downhill, just that and no more ...

I can't wait to settle down again to work in peace ... but it was necessary for me to show all I had till now accomplished in the miserable gloom of Milan, so that I could have the reassurance of seeing what point I had reached in my own revolution—and indeed all the people here who really know Italy and the infantile, ignoble, and vulgar condition of its esthetic ideals, are amazed that, struggling out of the Italian morass we should in one leap have set Italian art side by side with the art of France. The rest does not exist, as you know. In the past two years my production has aroused nothing but laughter, disdain and pity ...

I had hoped so much that you would come to Paris... You would have been amused to hear how people speak of me and what they expect of me!... It's somewhat frightening.

Never have I been so certain of the path I should follow as I am now! And what's more—I shall succeed!

Dearest Vico, these days I live on certainty, always heady food... At times I glance back on my past and with strange lucidity I feel the presence of those that were kind to me. While I remember others with hatred, I feel equivalent tenderness for the friends who sustained me in hard times.

In this spirit I shake hands and greet you.

Affectionate greetings to Mrs. Baer and Rupert

Paris, 15th March 1912

Dearest Vico,

Your letter is seasoned with the patronizing irony that seems the accepted way to address artists. I, however, am too certain of your friendship not to have smiled and yearned to be in Milan to talk psychology and philosophy with you just as you say!...

However, I confess that at the moment I am a bit worried because I cannot decide whether to settle down in Paris or come back to Italy. I am afraid that Milan would prove unbearable after the period, in fact the parenthesis, I have lived through in Paris—

I think I might be more advanced (though I may be wrong) if all the inner workings of my evolution had taken place in a more favorable climate such as that of Paris. I feel that many times I have lacked daring because of the spiritual isolation in which I lived. It was not only the solitude but the continuous corrosion of the indestructible core, now evolving according to its destiny, which contained the full impact of my discoveries in nature.

Paris and London were my proving grounds and now what I accomplished in Milan has taken on immense value in my eyes—not because of my works, I don't care about them—but because of the struggle for liberation and destruction that I undertook.

Now I wonder: what would I (perhaps) have done among people who *constantly* encouraged me? What would I have done if I had not always been faced with the fear of being thought a practical joker, a man on the wrong track, a brain that was going up in smoke?

My mind keeps harping on this and I confess that ten times a day I curse my lost time, my poverty, the cautiousness of my friends, the frightening emptiness of the Italian world! The passion to reacquire what I think I've lost and to strengthen what till now I doubted puts me in a rage against everyone!

I am obsessed these days by sculpture! I think I can perceive a complete renewal of this mummified art—

At the beginning of April I am leaving for Berlin where our exhibition is opening in galleries loaned to us by an avant-garde art association. From Berlin, alas, I shall come back directly to Milan—

Thereafter, the exhibition will go to Brussels.

Some American painters sent the catalogue with my preface back to New York and they tell me that the young artists are very enthusiastic and that in an art school a professor read the preface aloud and explained it to his students.

When I speak of those who understand I don't mean the 40,000 people who, according to the *Daily Mirror*, have seen the exhibition, *but those who perceive the symptoms that perhaps I alone have detected in art—I mean the seven or eight people who according to me are worthy of speaking of art....*

London, beautiful, monstrous, elegant, well-fed, well-dressed but with brains as heavy as steaks. Inside, the houses are magnificent: cleanliness, honesty, calm, order, but fundamentally these people are idiots or semi-idiots. When I think of all the socialist, co-operativist, positivist, hygienist imbecility that pretends to judge Italian things through the obsession of what is English, I feel nauseated. ... There is so much of Naples, so much raffishness in this marvelous Paris and it is from here that the light of the spirit will shine forth in the coming centuries!! Only here is there art, and art is the ultimate proof of the level of the people. What does it matter if some day under the ruins of London raincoats wil be excavated intact, and account books without ink spots? How many imbeciles there are in this world!

Café de la Paix

12, Bould. des Capucines, Paris.

[not dated]

First impressions after Paris opening (of sculpture show, June 1913)

I have not written sooner because I had nothing new to say. Dull waiting and customs trouble: yesterday was my opening. Lots of people, lots of drivel. The extent of my production amazes both friendly and hostile artists. Many are enthusiastic yet surprised, bewildered, uncertain. Sculpture is far less intellectual than painting. Those who can speak of it with competence are rare. Everyone is astonished by the number of works and by their daring. Apollinaire, completely pacified, is always with me. He wants me to cast many of my things in bronze as soon as I get back to Milan. He says there is no one left but me in modern sculpture. He says that

certain of my works are true historical documents that must be preserved. He wrote a little piece for the *Intransigeant* but today he is coming back to make a more serious study. He will give lectures in Italy.

He too is strangely taken aback by the intensity, the power, and the violence of my recent works, like a real bayonet attack!

Guillaume Apollinaire is completely won over to Futurism and soon we shall see results. He went on a lecture tour in Germany and he says that the influence and the renown of our painting is extraordinary. Yesterday evening we dined, he, Marinetti, and I in a celebrated restaurant on the "Rive Gauche." We argued from seven to three in the morning. We came away drunk and exhausted. After these debates where victory is won by magnetism—I find myself sad and discouraged. I wonder what I might have achieved by now if I had grown up in the atmosphere of Paris or Berlin... I certainly would not be in the forlorn condition in which Italy would abandon me; once in a while I take a great leap forward ... and this is what keeps me going.

Paris this time seems to have no hold on me, I feel that I have come with a kingdom of my own and I treat people here as my equals. I yearn for Milan, for my studio, though I dread the loneliness. However, I must go on!

All cubism does not seem to be going ahead by a single step, painting moves little and is surely not on the path of a true revolution of sensitivity. Archipenko's sculpture has lapsed into the archaic and the barbaric. This is a mistaken solution. Our own primitivism should have nothing in common with that of antiquity. Our primitivism is the extreme climax of *complexity*, whereas the primitivism of antiquity is the babbling of *simplicity*.

All this will be discussed in my book. Surely if my health and strength hold out I shall go far. I feel that I can do whatever I want!—

MOVIMENTO FUTURISTA—*diretto da F. T. Marinetti. Milano, Corso Venezia, 61*

[not dated]

Dear Vico!

Forgive the delay. I am in the middle of my work and I'm not in the mood to write. I don't feel very fit spiritually, I need great quiet and lots of work! The activity of my brain is such that when I put a stop to it, that is when I begin to work, I feel an unspeakable anxiety. Because, let's face it: *to create is to circumscribe, to create is relative,* whereas the mind lives in the intoxication of the absolute! ... It is terrible! ... *Especially for those who want to work!*

Best wishes,

Selected Bibliography of Futurism: 1905-1961

On this occasion it is possible to compile a limited bibliography which offers adequate guidance to the general public and to scholars. In 1958 Drudi Gambillo and Fiori (bibl. 75) published an exhaustive record on Futurism, including comprehensive reprints of manifestoes and similar documents. The following year, Falqui (bibl. 78) issued a work of equal stature covering not only the Futurist literature but art and music as well. Other sources of information — reported by Italians — are noted below: an unpublished typescript prepared by Scheiwiller (bibl. 40), Apollonio's continuing inventory in La Biennale (bibl. 49), Necchi and Giani in Carrieri's history (bibl. 42), and Aeschlimann's review of 1940–1952 editions (bibl. 53). Finally one can note the happy circumstance of an evaluated version of the fifty-seven page bibliography from the Archivi del Futurismo compressed into five pages for the Rome catalogue of 1959 (bibl. 79), and a cursory review of international commentary in La Biennale di Venezia (bibl. 76).

Where other references are lacking, certain surveys are still useful, such as the dictionaries of artists by Thieme and Becker and its modern complement by Vollmer (bibl. 56). Since the documentation in Skira's international enterprise, the *History of Modern Painting*, is largely the work of Hans Bolliger (bibl. 43), it constitutes a link between typical German studies, Degenhart (bibl. 68) and Haftmann (bibl. 61), and the *Amour de l'Art* anthology with "notices" by Germain Bazin (bibl. 33). Lately, *Cahiers d'Art* printed selected references in its Italian number (bibl. 45). American guides, to name but two, should include Clough's useful doctoral dissertation (bibl. 36) and the catalogue issued by The Museum of Modern Art for its show Twentieth-Century Italian Art (bibl. 41). Fortunately, English references continue to accumulate (bibl. 64), and translations have been noted on every occasion (bibl. 3, 9, 19, 36, 44; also 64, 67, 82, etc.).

In deference to Dr. Taylor's opinion that "most comments on futurism in recent publications … are of doubtful value" owing to "mis-information and a strongly French prejudice," this chronological listing of over 100 citations incorporates a few of his suggestions from the Italian literature and a selective inventory of titles already proved useful in the Library — presumably known and accessible to the public and student, here and elsewhere in the United States. For the convenience of the scholarly researcher, who will encounter frequent references to comparatively rare items in the major bibliographies, it can be mentioned that the Library can provide microfilm or photostat copies from the following: *Lacerba*, *Montjoie!*, *Les Soirées de Paris*, the early issues of *Der Sturm*, and, of course, representative Futurist manifestoes.

After the opening of the exhibition, lecturers may anticipate that lantern slides will be provided by the authorized agencies of the Museum: for black and white, Taurgo, and for color, Sandak.

BERNARD KARPEL
Librarian of the Museum

GENERAL REFERENCES (by date)

1 POESIA. Edited by Filippo Tommaso Marinetti. Milan, 1905–1909. *A literary journal of wide cultural interest, which published avant-garde poetry, and acted as pioneer publisher for early Futurism, including the manifestoes (bibl. 4) and an anthology (bibl. 7).*

2 LA VOCE. Edited by Giuseppe Prezzolini. Florence, 1908–1916. *Also edited for a short period by Giovanni Papini. Soffici associated as major art critic. For important articles, e. g. Roberto Longhi: Pittori futuristi (April 10, 1913) see notations in bibl. 76. "An important force in encouraging rebellion against tradition" (Taylor).*

3 MARINETTI, FILIPPO TOMMASO. Futurist manifesto (Feb. 20, 1909). *Architectural Review Aug. 1959. A "foundation document of extreme polemical violence," originally published in "Figaro" (Paris) and in range and variety of issue rivaling the Dada and Surrealist pronouncements. This is a complete English translation, accompanied by running commentary, by Reyner Banham. Also published here, p. 124–125.*

4 MANIFESTI DEL MOVIMENTO FUTURISTA: A Collection of Futurist Documents. [Milan, etc., Direzione del Movimento Futurista, 1909–192?]. *The Museum of Modern Art Library has assembled this representative collection in original (or photostat) for studying — in addition to content — typographical factors of style, scale, and layout. For dates see Taylor chronology; for supplemental details see Drudi Gambillo's chronological bibliography. Owing to the ephemeral nature of these leaflets, to their publication by chief or lesser figures, to their issuance as individual, group or anonymous statements, and to variations in time and place, the term "Futurist manifesto" has a certain flexibility. These broadsides were issued initially by "Poesia," then by the "Movimento Futurista," and after Jan. 1913, by "Lacerba." Most were republished either by that magazine or other contemporaneous journals, and in collections, notably Marinetti*

(bibl. 13). The Archivi (bibl. 75) includes a classified arrangement of 26 manifestoes.

5 APOLLINAIRE, GUILLAUME. Les Peintres futuristes. Mercure de France Nov. 16, 1911. Reprinted in "Anecdotiques" (bibl. 62) which includes similar hard-to-find texts from Feb. 16, 1912, Oct. 16, 1913, Feb. 1, 1914, Oct. 16, 1916.

6 MARINETTI, FILIPPO TOMMASO. Le Futurisme. Paris, Sansot [1911]. Usually so noted, although "1910" is mentioned by Clough. The 5th ed. (n.d.) in the Library includes "manifestes et proclamations futuristes."

7 MARINETTI, FILIPPO TOMMASO. I Poeti Futuristi. Milan, Ed. Futuriste de "Poesia," 1912. An anthology of Futurist poetry, with an important preface by Marinetti.

8 BERNHEIM-JEUNE ET CIE. Les Peintres Futuristes Italiens: Boccioni, Carrà, Russolo, Balla, Severini. Paris, 1912. Includes catalogue of show held Feb. 5–24, "les exposants au public," "manifeste des peintres futuristes." Similar catalogues issued for European tour, "Der Sturm" (Berlin), etc. Reproduced with itinerary in Boccioni, 1914 (bibl. 14). An important review of the Amsterdam exhibition (Huneker, bibl. 29) is not reported in "Archivi del Futurismo."

9 SACKVILLE GALLERY. Exhibition of Works of the Italian Futurist Painters. London, 1912. Catalogue of 34 works in March show (with annotations), the "Initial Manifesto of Futurism," "The Exhibitors to The Public," "Technical Manifesto: Futurist Painters." Also reprinted here, p. 124–129.

10 DER STURM. Edited by Herwarth Walden. Berlin, 1912–13. Manifestoes, illustrations, and other items by and on the Futurists appeared in these early numbers: 101, 104, 105, 107, 111, 112, 132, 133, 136, 137 (1912); 150, 151, 172, 173, 190, 191 (1913). For supplemental data on Der Sturm Gallery, its exhibitions and publications see bibl. 21, 57.

11 MAYAKOVSKY, VLADIMIR. Theatre, cinema, futurism. Kine Journal. July 27, 1913. Reprinted in Jay Leyda: Kino, a History of the Russian and Soviet Film, p. 412–413 (London, 1960). Several early Russian references are recorded by Drudi Gambillo (bibl. 75).

12 LACERBA. Edited by Giovanni Papini. Florence, no. 1–22, 1913–1915. A futurist journal founded by Papini, Soffici, Palazzeschi and Tavolato. Includes illustrations, articles, and manifestoes, most of which are reprinted, fortunately, in the "Archivi" (bibl. 75). Also note bibl. 78.

13 MARINETTI, FILIPPO TOMMASO, ed. I Manifesti del Futurismo. Florence, Ed. di "Lacerba," 1914. "Lanciatta da Marinetti, Boccioni, Carrà, Russolo, Balla, Severini, Pratella, Mme de Saint-Point, Apollinaire, Palazzeschi." A major anthology of the manifestoes published prior to 1914. Also note reprints in the "Archivi" (bibl. 75), and other editions (Milan, 1919, etc.).

14 BOCCIONI, UMBERTO. Pittura, Scultura Futuriste. Dinamismo Plastico. Milan, Ed. Futuriste di "Poesia," 1914. Written 1913, published March 1914. Manifesto, p. 337–449. Opere futuriste (in touring exhibitions), p. 457–469. Reprint, omitting illustrations and manifestoes issued

as: Estetica e Arte Futuriste (Milan, Il Balcone, 1946). Boccioni's ideas are expounded, and words comprehensively translated, in Clough (bibl. 36).

15 COQUIOT, GUSTAVE. Cubistes, Futuristes, Passéistes. Essai Sur la Jeune Peinture et la Jeune Sculpture. Paris, Ollendorf [1914]. On Futurist painting and Boccioni. New edition 1923.

16 EDDY, ARTHUR J. Cubists and Post-Impressionism. Chicago, McClurg, 1914. Comments on, quotes from the Futurists, p. 164–190. Bibliography in English, French, German. Revised edition 1919.

17 LEWIS, WYNDHAM. The melodrama of modernity. Blast no. 1: 143–144 June 20, 1914. Also "Marinetti's occupation" (no. 2: 26) and "A review of contemporary art" (no. 2: 36ff), July 1915. Compare "Vital English art" by Marinetti and Nevinson in "Lacerba," 2 no. 4: 209–210, July 15, 1914.

18 PAPINI, GIOVANNI. L'Esperienza Futurista. 1913–1914. Florence, Vallecchi, 1919. Second edition 1927. Also: Il Mio Futurismo. Florence, Ed. di "Lacerba," 1914.

19 TRASK, JOHN E. D. and LAURVIK, J. N., ed. Catalogue de luxe of the Department of Fine Arts, Panama–Pacific International Exposition. San Francisco, Elder, 1915. Includes Boccioni: The Italian Futurist painters and sculptors (p. 123–127).

20 WRIGHT, WILLARD H. Modern Painting — Its Tendency and Meaning, p. 263–276. New York, London: John Lane, 1915. Also 1926 edition.

21 WALDEN, HERWARTH. Einblick in Kunst: Expressionismus, Futurismus, Kubismus. Berlin, Verlag der Sturm, 1917. Boccioni and illustrative material; various editions to 1924. Also note bibl. 57.

22 MARINETTI, FILIPPO TOMMASO. Les Mots en Liberté Futuristes. Milan, Ed. Futuriste di "Poesia," 1919. Includes specimens of Futurist typography and layout.

23 HUELSENBECK, RICHARD. En Avant Dada. Eine Geschichte des Dadaismus. Hannover, etc., Steegemann, 1920. Translated in The Dada Painters and Poets, p. 24–27 (bibl. 52).

24 SOFFICI, ARDENGO. Primi Principi di una Estetica Futurista. Florence, Vallechi, 1920. Reprinted in "Archivi del Futurismo" (bibl. 75).

25 PRAMPOLINI, ENRICO. The aesthetic of the machine and mechanical introspection in art. Little Review 10 no. 2: 49–51. Autumn-Winter 1924–25. Also published in "Broom" 3 no. 235–237 (1922). His "Manifesto dell'estetica della machina" is discussed in Clough (bibl. 36), and similarly for "post-war Futurism" as a whole.

26 FLORA, FRANCESCO. Dal Romanticismo al Futurismo. Milan, Mondadori, 1925. Largely, but not entirely, a critique of the error of Futurist theory. See comprehensive summary in Clough, ch. 7 (bibl. 36).

27 EINSTEIN, CARL. Die Kunst des 20. Jahrhunderts. Berlin, Propyläen, 1926. Second edition 1928; third revision, 1931. Includes illustrations and biographical notes.

28 FILLIA (ENRICO COLOMBO). Il Futurismo. Milan, Sonzogno, 1932. "Ideologie, realizzazioni, e polemiche del movimento," with many manifestoes, in whole or part. His

"La Nuova Architettura" (Turin, 1931) includes architectural manifestoes.

29 HUNEKER, JAMES G. Ivory, Apes and Peacocks. New York, Scribner's Sons, 1932. *"The Italian Futurist painters," p. 262–274, comments on the exhibition seen at the De Roos Gallery, Amsterdam, Sept. 1912.*

30 MARINETTI, FILIPPO TOMMASO. Il futurismo. *In* Enciclopedia Italiana, vol. 16. Rome, Trecanni, 1932. *Note other entries under personalities in this well-illustrated and documented encyclopedia (1929–1949). Clough records "Futurism to 1933" as a contemporaneous essay issued by the "Chicago Tribune" in an Italian supplement of 1933.*

31 COSTANTINI, VINCENZO. Pittura Italiana Contemporanea. Milan, Hoepli, 1932. *"Il futurismo," p. 183–208; documentation, p. 387 ff. Similar works: Scultura e Pittura Italiana (1940), etc.*

32 AMOUR DE L'ART. Paris, Nov. 1934. *Special Italian number of vol. 15 (p. 469–491) incorporated into annual issued by Alcan below, with text by Costantini and others.*

33 HUYGHE RENÉ, ed. Histoire de l'Art Contemporain: la Peinture. Paris, Alcan, 1935. *Articles by Huyghe, Severini, Vergnet-Ruiz, Costantini; extensive biographical and bibliographical notes by G. Bazin from bibl. 32.*

34 BARR, ALFRED H., JR. Cubism and Abstract Art. New York, The Museum of Modern Art, 1936. *History and exhibition catalogue, p. 54–63, 205 et passim.*

35 LEMAITRE, GEORGES. From Cubism to Surrealism in French Literature. Cambridge, Harvard University Press, 1941. *Futurism discussed p. 148–153, and in later edition (1947).*

36 CLOUGH, ROSA TRILLO. Looking Back at Futurism. New York (Cocce Press for the author) 1942. *An outstanding dissertation on the writings and theories of the Futurists, emphasizing literary aspects, with extensive quotation and translations from Marinetti, Boccioni, etc. Contents: Introduction — Italy: 1900–1914. — I. Revolt against the past. — II. Literature. — III. Painting. — IV. Sculpture. — V. Architecture. — VI. Post-war Futurism. — Bibliography (p. 205–207.)*

37 CAIROLA, STEFANO, ed. Arte Italiana del Nostro Tempo. Bergamo, Istituto Italiano d'Arte Grafiche, 1946. *Pictorial anthology with biographical sections. Data on Carrà, Rosai, Severini, Sironi, Soffici.*

38 SMITH, HORATIO, ed. Columbia Dictionary of Modern European Literature. New York, Columbia University Press, 1947. *Excellent résumés on Marinetti by R. Morand, on Italian literature and Papini by G. Prezzolini, etc. Bibliographies.*

39 SOBY, JAMES T. Contemporary Painters. New York, The Museum of Modern Art, 1948. *Reprints, p. 104–114, essay from the "Magazine of Art" (Feb. 1946) on Boccioni and de Chirico.*

40 SCHEIWILLER, GIOVANNI. Arte Moderna Italiana (bibliografia). 73 leaves. Milan, 1949. *Extensive typescript compiled by an eminent bibliographer and writer on the occasion of the Museum of Modern Art show (bibl. 41). General and individual references; additional data in Hoepli's series "Arte Moderna Italiana" and elsewhere.*

41 SOBY, JAMES T. & BARR, ALFRED H., JR. Twentieth Century Italian Art. New York, Museum of Modern Art, 1949. *Essays, including Barr on "early futurism" and catalogue of exhibition; bibliography by B. Karpel, p. 136–144.*

42 CARRIERI, RAFFAELE. Pittura, Scultura d'Avanguardia (1890–1950) in Italia. Milan, Conchiglia, 1950. *Futurism, p. 17–85 followed by comprehensive survey, with extensive documentation by Elda Necchi and Vrania Giani. Also revised edition 1955 (bibl. 64).*

43 RAYNAL, MAURICE [and others]. History of Modern Painting, [vol. 3]: From Picasso to Surrealism. Geneva, Skira, 1950. *Futurism reviewed briefly (p. 82–85) as a reaction to cubism; biographical notes on Boccioni, Carrà, Severini. Published in French, German and in compressed edition (one vol.) as "Modern Painting" (1953, reprint 1956). Documentation by Hans Bolliger and others.*

44 RITCHIE, ANDREW C. Sculpture of the Twentieth Century, New York, The Museum of Modern Art, 1950. *Based on Museum exhibition, section on "the object dissected" (p. 25–28); quotes Boccioni (p. 41–42).*

45 ZERVOS, CHRISTIAN, ed. Un Semi-Siècle d'Art Italian. Paris, Cahiers d'Art, 1950. *Special number of "Cahiers d'Art," vol. 25 (276 p.), numerous illustrations and selected bibliography. Manifestoes by Boccioni, Carrà, Russolo, Severini and others, texts by Marinetti, Zervos, F. Pastorichi. Important "Souvenirs sur le futurisme" by Paolo Buzzi and documentation and chronological exposition, "Le futurisme" by Benedetta Marinetti. Some errors in chronology.*

46 ZEVI, BRUNO. Storia dell'Architettura Moderna. Turin, Einaudi, 1950. *On Futurism and Sant'Elia (p. 221–231) including bibliography. Revised edition 1953. Also note bibl. 100.*

47 VENICE. ESPOSIZIONE BIENNALE INTERNAZIONALE D'ARTE. Catalogo. Venice, 1950. *Sala VI—Umbro Apollonio: I firmatari del primo manifesto futurista (p. 55–58). Also G. C. Argan: Aspects of the Venice biennale: futurism. "Burlington Magazine" 92:265–266 Sept. 1950.*

48 ZURICH. KUNSTHAUS. Futurismo e Pittura Metafisica. Zurich, 1950. *Catalogue with bibliography (p. 33–34). Reviews: "Emporium" 113:139 (1951), "Panorama dell'Arte Italiana" p. 13–15 (1951), "Werk" 38: suppl. 3–4 (Jan. 1951).*

49 LA BIENNALE DI VENEZIA. Venice, No. 1, July 1950—current. *Comprehensive bibliography included in regular report of library acquisitions by Umbro Apollonio: "Bollettino dell'archivo storico d'arte contemporanea."*

50 SPAZIO. Rome, No. 1, July 1950. *Includes, in addition to illustrations, "Omaggio a Boccioni" by C. Zervos and M. Sironi, and "Valore storico del futurismo" by A. Soffici. English résumé.*

51 CURJEL, HANS. Bemerkungen zum Futurismus. *Das Kunstwerk 5 no. 3 1951. Critical article, p. 5–13; reproduces 3 manifestoes in French.*

52 MOTHERWELL, ROBERT, ed. The Dada Painters and Poets: an Anthology. New York, Wittenborn, Schultz, 1951. *Translations and extracts from the Dadaist literature,*

1914–1951, for example, bibl. 23. See index on Boccioni, Marinetti, Futurism, etc. Extensive bibliography.

53 AESCHLIMANN, ERARDO, ed. Bibliografia del Libro d'Arte Italiano, 1940–1952. Rome, Bestetti, 1952.

54 SEVERINI, GINO. Apollinaire et le futurisme. *XXe Siècle no. 3 June 1952. For Apollinaire's position see his "Anecdotiques" (bibl. 62) Calvesi (bibl. 75, p. 21–44) and Dr. Taylor's footnote 27.*

55 VENTURI, LIONELLO. Italian Painting from Caravaggio to Modigliani. Geneva, Skira, 1952. *Futurism, p. 129–141 (Boccioni, Carrà, Balla, Severini); surveys by R. Skira-Venturi; bibliography by E. Battisti. Also French edition.*

56 VOLLMER, HANS, ed. Allgemeines Lexikon der Bildenden Künstler des XX. Jahrhunderts. 4 vol. (to date) Leipzig, Seemann, 1953–1959. *Includes bibliography, also supplemented by older data in Thieme-Becker's "Künstler-Lexikon" (1907–1950) in which Vollmer collaborated.*

57 WALDEN, NELL & SCHREYER, LOTHAR. Der Sturm. Baden Baden, Klein, 1954. *Includes H. Walden's memoir on Boccioni and an index to "Der Sturm" (bibl. 10).*

58 BARR, ALFRED H., JR. Masters of Modern Art. New York, Museum of Modern Art, 1954. *Selected Futurist high points in the collection, p. 98–102.*

59 DORAZIO, PIERO. The future that ended in 1915. *Art News Jan. 1954. Commentary on show at the Rose Fried Gallery, New York (52:54–55, 84–86). Also note preface by Lionello Venturi to that gallery's catalogue ("The futurists: Balla, Severini, 1912–1918") and W. Rubin's review in the "Art Digest" (28:13–14 Feb. 1, 1954).*

60 JANIS, SIDNEY, GALLERY. Futurism. New York, 1954. *Catalogue includes Balla, Boccioni, Carrà, Russolo, with excerpt from his "Abstract and Surrealist Art in America" (N.Y., Reynal & Hitchcock, 1944). For review by T. B. Hess see "Art News," Apr. 1954 (53:44).*

61 HAFTMANN, WERNER. Malerei im 20. Jahrhundert. 2 vol. Munich, Prestel, 1954–1955. *Survey (p. 157–164), biographical notes and plates. Revised English edition in preparation. (New York, Abrams, 1961?)*

62 APOLLINAIRE, GUILLAUME. Anecdotiques. Paris, Gallimard, 1955. *Includes otherwise inaccessible essays and reviews from 1911, 1912, 1913, 1914, 1916 (p. 49–50, 64, 141–145, 121–123, 127–128, 218–223, 291–292, 304–305). In 1926 edition see p. 45–46. For associated references, bibl. 54.*

63 BANHAM, REYNER. Futurism. *Art (London) Mar. 3, 1955. V. 1, no. 8: 6–7; opening of a continuing exposition followed by bibl. 70, 77, 82, 87.*

64 CARRIERI, RAFFAELE. Avant-garde Painting and Sculpture (1890–1955) in Italy, Milan, Domus, 1955. *Revised version of the Conchiglia text of 1950 (bibl. 42). Includes partial English translations, additional color plates, omits Italian bibliography.*

65 GIEDION-WELCKER, CAROLA. Contemporary Sculpture: An Evolution in Volume and Space. New York, Wittenborn, 1955. *Text (p. XIII–XIV) and annotated plates (p. 76–81); biography (p. 260) and bibliography on Boccioni. Also German edition, supplemented by essay in "Werk" (Nov. 1950): Vergängliches und Zukünftiges im Futurismus*

(37: 345–353), *reprinted in Winterthur catalogue (bibl. 79).*

66 LAKE, CARLTON & MAILLARD, ROBERT. Dictionary of Modern Painting. New York, Paris Book Center, 1955. *Translation of Hazan edition (Paris), also published by Knaur (Munich). Includes Balla, Boccioni, Carrà, Severini, and contributions by M. Seuphor.*

67 BALLO, GUIDO. Pittori Italiani del Futurismo a Oggi. Rome, Ed. Mediterranée, 1956. *Bibliography omitted from revised English edition: "Modern Italian Painting from Futurism to the Present Day," New York, Praeger, 1958. Includes: Futurism, Boccioni, La Voce and Lacerba, Severini (p. 14–31), and chronological survey (p. 207 ff).*

68 DEGENHART, BERNHARD. Italienische Zeichner der Gegenwart. Berlin, Mann, 1956. *With selective bibliography (p. 59–61) and artist references.*

69 SEUPHOR, MICHEL. Le futurisme … hier. *L'Oeil Feb. 1956. Illustrated essay (no. 14 : 32–39, 44) translated in "The Selective Eye, 1956–1957" (p. 96–103) Paris, Lausanne, Bernier; N.Y., Raynal, 1956.*

70 BANHAM, REYNER. Futurism and modern architecture. *Royal Institute of British Architects Journal Feb. 1957. The complete article (64: 129–139) includes the manifesto of Futurist architecture and a discussion. Banham has referred to the "Messagio sull'architettura moderna" in "Revista Tecnica (Lugano)," no. 7 1956, as the authoritative text established by Bernasconi and translated in bibl. 82 (p. 128–130).*

71 ROME, GALLERIA NAZIONALE D'ARTE MODERNA. Scultura Italiana del XX Secolo. Rome, Editalia, 1957. *Preface by Palma Bucarelli for Oct.–Nov. show; catalogue by G. Carandente (p. 2–39).*

72 SELZ, PETER. German Expressionist Painting. Berkeley & Los Angeles, University of California Press, 1957. *On the "introduction of Futurism into Germany," p. 258 ff.*

73 SEUPHOR, MICHEL. Dictionary of Abstract Painting. New York, Paris Book Center, 1957. *"With a history of abstract painting." Translated from the Hazan edition (Paris). Sections on Balla, Boccioni, Severini; bibliography (p. 297–304).*

74 MODESTI, RENZO. Pittura Italiana Contemporanea. Milan, Vallardi, 1958. *"Il futurismo," p. 9–26; also documentation on Balla, Boccioni, Rosai, Russolo, Severini, Sironi, Soffici (p. 181 ff).*

75 DRUDI GAMBILLO, MARIA & FIORI, TERESA. Archivi del Futurismo. Rome, De Luca, 1958. *A monumental anthology (618 p.) including a comprehensive chronological bibliography (p. 497–553). As the first of 2 vol. in the "Archivi dell'Arte Contemporanea," it includes manifestoes, extracts from catalogues, statements by artists, letters by personalities, biographical notes, list of works, and chronology (1909–1921). The bibliography records items until 1957; a selective version appeared in bibl. 79 (including some references in 1958–59) and an abbreviated international review by the same compiler in "La Biennale" (bibl. 76, p. 54 ff.).*

76 LA BIENNALE DI VENEZIA, July–Dec. 1959. *Entire issue*

on Futurism (9 no. 36–37; 3–87) including important articles by P. Francastel, M. Calvesi, M. Drudi Gambillo ("La critica dei contemporanei," 1910–1926, p. 54–59), G. Mazzariol, C. Bo, G. Samonà, P. Schaeffer, C. Molinari, G. Aristarco, A. G. Bragaglia.

77 BANHAM, REYNER. Futurist manifesto. *Architectural Review* Aug. 1959. *Marinetti's major pronouncement of Feb. 20, 1909 in a complete English translation, accompanied by introduction and running commentary (126: 77–80).*

78 FALQUI, ENRICO. Bibliografia e Iconografia del Futurismo. Florence, Sansoni, 1959. *Biblioteca bibliografica italica, v. 21 (239 p.). Extensive coverage on art, literature, music, with useful illustrations and facsimiles. Previously published: "Indici di Lacerba" (Rome, 1938).*

79 ROME, ENTE PREMI ROMA. Il Futurismo. Rome, De Luca, 1959. *"Presentazione di Aldo Palazzeschi. Saggi critici di Giorgio Castelfranco e Jacopo Recupero. Catalogo, regesti e bibliografia di Laura (Maria) Drudi Gambillo. Bibliografia essenziale." (p. 93–96), based on the "Archivi del Futurismo," but includes some 1958–59 citations. 214 works, 38 plates, 5 col. pl., biographical notes. Exhibited at the Palazzo Barberini; shown Oct. 4 – Nov. 15 at the Winterthur Kunstverein, with modified catalogue (38 p.), preface by C. Giedion-Welcker.*

80 SEUPHOR, MICHEL. La Sculpture de Ce Siècle. Neuchâtel, Griffin, 1959. *Includes chapters on Boccioni and other Italians, with documentation. English edition: "The Sculpture of This Century" (N.Y., Braziller, 1960).*

81 VACCARI, WALTER. Vita e Tumulti di Marinetti. Milan, Omnia, 1959.

82 BANHAM, REYNER. Theory and Design in the First Machine Age. London, Architectural Press; New York, Praeger, 1960. *"Section 2 — Italy: Futurist manifestoes and projects, 1909–1914" includes theory, history and Sant'Elia. Reprints, in English, the text of "Messagio sull'Architettura moderna" (Rivista Tecnica, Lugano, no. 7, 1956). Bibliography.*

83 ENCYCLOPEDIA OF WORLD ART, 15 vol. New York, McGraw-Hill, 1960 — in progress. *American revision of edition being published by the Istituto per la Collaborazione Culturale (Rome & Venice). To include articles on Balla, Boccioni, Carrà, Futurism, etc., with bibliographies. Vol. 1 and 2 issued 1960.*

84 MARINETTI, F. T. Teatro Completo. 3 v. Milan, Omnia, 1960.

85 NEW YORK. MUSEUM OF MODERN ART, INTERNATIONAL COUNCIL. Arte Italiana del XX Secolo da Collezioni Americane. Milan, Silvana, 1960. *Introduction by J. T. Soby. Works shown Milan and Rome, include Balla (no. 8–18), Boccioni (no. 22–46), Carrà (no. 60–68), Russolo (no. 164–165), Severini (no. 172–178), Sironi (no. 179–182), Soffici (no. 183). Plates, p. 24–69.*

86 VENICE. ESPOSIZIONE BIENNALE INTERNAZIONALE D'ARTE. Catalogo. Venice, 1960. *Included "Mostra storico del futurismo," with preface by Guido Ballo (p. 6–13), list of 143 works and plates 1–43.*

87 BANHAM, REYNER. Futurism for keeps. *Arts (New York)* 35 no. 3: 33–39 Dec. 1960.

88 PARIS. MUSÉE D'ART MODERNE. Les Sources du XXe Siècle: les Arts en Europe de 1884 à 1914. Paris, 1960. *Major catalogue for exhibit held Nov. 4, 1960 – Jan. 23, 1961. Preface by C. C. Argan; also notes on Balla, Boccioni, Carrà, Severini, Sironi, Soffici, etc.*

89 DORAZIO, VIRGINIA DORTCH, ed. Futurballa. New York, Wittenborn [1961?]. *In active preparation. "English text. Photographic survey of the Futurists at work, their studios and friends."*

INDIVIDUAL REFERENCES

Owing to limitations of space as well as opportunity to evaluate the extensive documentation already reported above, the following is restricted to a few works suggested by Dr. Taylor. The most convenient point to start bibliographical research is the alphabetical listing in Carrieri (bibl. 42) which includes all but three artists in this exhibition. Dudreville and Giannattasio can be extracted from the Archivi (bibl. 75) and Sant'Elia is adequately presented in Zevi (bibl. 46), comprehensively in the Archivi and exhaustively in La Martinella (bibl. 100).

Balla

90 MARCHI, VIRGILIO. Giacomo Balla. *La Stirpe (Rome)* Mar. 1928.

Boccioni

91 BOCCIONI, UMBERTO. Opera Completa. Foligno, Campitelli, 1927. *Edited by F. T. Marinetti.*

92 PEROCCO, GUIDO, ed. I Primi Espositori di Ca'Pesaro, 1908–1919. Venice, 1958. *Includes Boccioni's letters to Barbantini.*

93 ARGAN, GIULIO CARLO. Umberto Boccioni. Rome, De Luca, 1953. *"Scelta degli scritti, regesti, bibliografia e catalogo delle opere a cura di Maurizio Calvesi."*

94 LONGHI, ROBERTO. Scultura Futurista: Boccioni. Florence, La Voce, 1915.

95 CALVESI, MAURIZIO. Il futurismo di Boccioni: formazione e tempi. *Arte Antica e Moderna* 2: 149–169 April – June 1958.

Carrà

96 CARRÀ, CARLO. La Mia Vita. Rome, Longanesi, 1943.

97 PACCHIONI, GUGLIELMO. Carlo Carrà. Milan, Ed. del Milione, 1945. *Extensive bibliography.*

Rosai

98 ROSAI, OTTONE. Vecchio Autoritratto, Florence, Vallecchi, 1951.

Sant'Elia

99 APOLLONIO, UMBRO. Antonio Sant'Elia. Milan, Il Balcone, 1958. *"Documenti e disegni raccolti e commentati da Leonardo Mariani."*

100 LA MARTINELLA DI MILANO. Oct. 1958. *Special Sant'Elia number (12 no. 10: 523–543) with several articles and extensive bibliography.*

Severini

101 SEVERINI, GINO. Tutta la Vita di un Pittore. Milan, Garzanti, 1946.

Soffici

102 SOFFICI, ARDENGO. Ricordi di Vita Artistica e Letteraria. Florence, Vallecchi, 1930. *Also 1942 edition.*

103 SOFFICI, ARDENGO. Opere, I. Florence, Vallecchi, 1959.

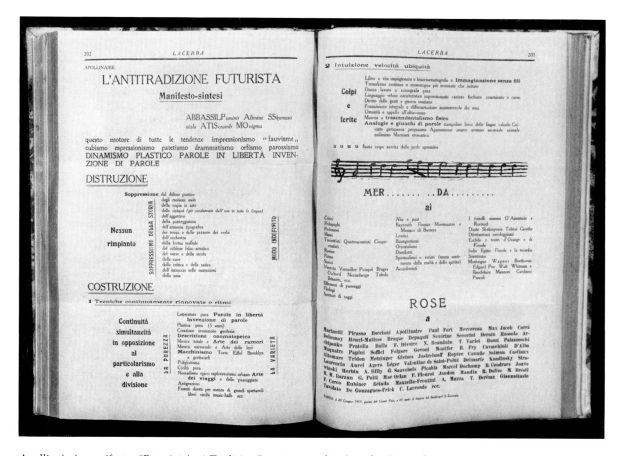

Apollinaire's manifesto, "Futurist Anti-Tradition," as it appeard in *Lacerba*, September 15, 1913

Biographies and Catalogue of the Exhibition

Works marked with an asterisk are illustrated. Dates enclosed in parentheses do not appear on the works of art. In dimensions, height precedes width.

GIACOMO BALLA

Born Turin, August 18, 1871; died Rome, March 5, 1958

After a period of study in evening classes in Turin, Balla moved in 1893 to Rome, which remained the center of his activity for the rest of his life. In 1900 he spent seven months in Paris. On his return he became the teacher of both Severini and Boccioni, introducing them to the divisionist techniques of which he had become the master. With them he signed the Futurist manifesto of February 1910, although his first clearly Futurist works date from 1912. In that year he spent some time in Düsseldorf, painting and designing the decorations of a music room. His skill as a designer is evident in many of his later works which had great influence on the second phase of Futurism. In the mid-1930s Balla turned to figurative painting in a somewhat impressionist manner.

*1 *Work (Lavoro).* Signed lower left, "Balla 1902." Oil on canvas, 68³/₄×49¹/₄". Collection Mr. and Mrs. Harry Lewis Winston, Birmingham, Michigan. Ill. p. 18.

*2 *Bankrupt (Fallimento).* Signed lower right, "Balla 1902." Oil on canvas, 46¹/₂×63¹/₄". Collection Dr. Giuseppe Cosmelli, Rome. Ill. p. 19.

*3 *The Stairway of Farewells (Gli addii scala).* (1908). Signed lower right, "Balla." Oil on canvas, 41¹/₂×41¹/₂". Collection Mr. and Mrs. Harry Lewis Winston, Birmingham, Michigan. This painting was exhibited in Rome in the 80th International Exhibition of the *Amatori e Cultori di Belle Arti,* 1910. Ill. p. 15.

*4 *The Street Light—Study of Light (Lampada—Studio di luce).* Dated upper left, "AN 1909"; signed lower right, "Balla." Oil on canvas, 68³/₄×45¹/₄". The Museum of Modern Art, New York. Hillman Periodicals Fund. Listed in the catalogue of the Bernheim-Jeune exhibition, 1912, but probably was not shown. Ill. p. 26.

*5 *Girl Running on a Balcony (Bambina che corre sul balcone).* Signed lower right, "1912 Balla." Oil on canvas, 49¹/₄×49¹/₄". Civica Galleria d'Arte Moderna, Milan. Grassi Collection. Exhibited in Rome in February 1913 at the Teatro Costanzi, and in Rotterdam in May of the same year. Ill. p. 60.

*6 *Rhythm of the Violinist (Ritmo del violinista).* (1912). Signed bottom center, "Balla." Oil on canvas, 20¹/₂ ×29¹/₂". Collection Eric Estorick, London. Painted in Düsseldorf, 1912. Balla made three trips to Düsseldorf, the first in 1912, where he decorated the music room in the home of a former pupil, a Hungarian girl who had married a lawyer named Loewenstein. Mr. Loewenstein was an amateur musician and served as inspiration for this painting. Exhibited in Rome in February 1913 at the Teatro Costanzi, and in Rotterdam in May of the same year. Ill. p. 59.

*7 *Iridescent Interpenetration (Compenetrazione iridescente).* Signed lower left, "Balla 1912," (on vertical). Oil on canvas, 39³/₈×23⁵/₈". Collection Mr. and Mrs. Harry Lewis Winston, Birmingham, Michigan. This is one of several paintings based on studies begun in Düsseldorf in 1912. Ill. p. 62.

8 *Iridescent Interpenetration (Compenetrazione iridescente),* No. 8. (1912). Watercolor, 12⁵/₈×13". Collection Hon. Pietro Campilli, Rome.

9 *Speeding Automobile (Automobile in corsa).* Signed lower left, "Fut Balla 1912." Oil on wood, 21⁷/₈×27¹/₈". The Museum of Modern Art, New York. Purchase.

*10 *Abstract Speed—Wake of Speeding Automobile (Velocità astratta—l'auto è passata).* (1913). Signed lower left, "Futur/Balla." Oil on canvas, 20¹/₈×25¹/₂". Collection Hon. Pietro Campilli, Rome. Ill. p. 64.

*11 *Speed of an Automobile+Lights (Velocità d'automobile + luci).* (1913). Signed lower left, "Balla." Oil on cardboard, 19×26³/₄". Collection Mr. and Mrs. Morton G. Neumann, Chicago. Ill. p. 64.

12 *Automobile + Speed + Lights (Automobile + velocità + luci).* Signed lower left, "Futur Balla 1913." Charcoal, 26³/₈×34⁵/₈". Collection Dr. Riccardo Jucker, Milan.

*13 *Flight of Swifts (Volo di rondoni).* Signed lower right, "Balla 1913." Oil on canvas, 16¹/₂×20⁷/₈". Collection Hon. Pietro Campilli, Rome. Ill. p. 63.

*14 *Swifts: Paths of Movement+Dynamic Sequences (Volo di rondoni).* Signed lower left, "Fut Balla 1913" (on vertical). Oil on canvas, 38¹/₈×47¹/₄". The Museum of Modern Art, New York. Purchase. Ill. p. 63.

15 *Vortex (Vortice).* (1913). Signed lower left, "Futur Balla/ Vortice." Oil on paper, mounted on white linen, 25¹/₂ ×32¹/₂". Coll. Mr. and Mrs. Joseph Slifka, New York.

*16 *Mercury Passing Before the Sun as Seen Through a Telescope (Mercurio che passa davanti al sole visto col cannocchiale).* Signed lower left, "Balla 1914." Tempera

141

on paper, $47^{1}/_{4} \times 39^{3}/_{8}$". Collection Dr. Gianni Mattioli, Milan. This is one of several versions of this subject. Ill. p. 65.

17 *Crowd and Landscape (Folla e paesaggio)*. Signed lower center, "Balla Futurista 1915." Collage, $60 \times 26^{1}/_{4}$". Collection Mr. and Mrs. Harry Lewis Winston, Birmingham, Michigan.

*18 *Boccioni's Fist—Lines of Force (Il pugno di Boccioni—linee di forza)*. (1915). Cardboard and wood, painted red, 33" high. Collection Mr. and Mrs. Harry Lewis Winston, Birmingham, Michigan. Recently casts in bronze have been made from this work. All of Balla's sculpture was originally made from insubstantial material, and few pieces now remain. Ill. p. 117.

19 *Spring (Primavera)*. (c. 1916). Signed lower right, "Balla Futur. . . ." Oil on canvas, $32 \times 26^{1}/_{2}$". The Museum of Modern Art, New York. Gift of Mr. and Mrs. Arnold H. Maremont.

*20 *The Injection of Futurism (Iniezione di futurismo)*. (c. 1918). Signed lower right, "Iniezione di Futurismo/Balla Futurista." Oil on canvas, $31^{3}/_{4} \times 45^{1}/_{4}$". Collection Mr. and Mrs. Harry Lewis Winston, Birmingham, Michigan. Ill. p. 16.

UMBERTO BOCCIONI

Born Reggio Calabria, October 19, 1882, of parents from Romagna; died Verona, August 17, 1916.

As a child Boccioni moved with his family to Forlì, then Genoa, and finally Padua. In 1897 he accompanied his father to Sicily where he completed his studies at the Technical Institute in Catania. In order to study painting, with which his father was not in sympathy, Boccioni moved to Rome in 1898. He lived in the home of his father's sister while studying in the life classes at the academy. In Rome he knew Severini and Sironi, and with the former studied in the studio of Balla about 1901. In 1902, with the prize money from a work shown in Rome, he went to Paris where he spent several months. In 1904 he made a trip to Russia with a family he had met in Paris. From 1905 through 1907 he worked in Padua and Venice, then moved to Milan where, in 1909, he met Marinetti and became an active member of the Futurist circle. Certainly the two painting manifestoes of 1910 owe most to Boccioni's pen. To his activity as painter he added that of sculptor in 1912. In 1915 he enlisted with other Futurists in the volunteer corps of the army and served on the Italian front. Released after a few months, he returned to painting, following a style much closer to that of Cézanne. He was recalled to military service in 1916 and, during a cavalry exercise on August 16, was mortally injured when knocked from a horse.

21 *Self Portrait (Autoritratto)*. (c. 1907). Signed lower right, "Boccioni." Oil on canvas, $20^{1}/_{4} \times 27$". Collection Mr. and Mrs. Harry Lewis Winston, Birmingham, Michigan.

*22 *Portrait of the Sculptor, Brocchi (Ritratto dello scultore Brocchi)*. (1907). Oil on canvas, $41^{3}/_{4} \times 49^{5}/_{8}$". Collection Dr. Paolo Marinotti. Ill. p. 24.

*23 *Self Portrait (Autoritratto)*. Signed upper right, "U Boccioni 1908." Oil on canvas, $27^{1}/_{2} \times 39^{3}/_{8}$" Pinacoteca di Brera, Milan. Ill. p. 24.

*24 Study for *Mourning (Studio per Lutto)*. (1910). Signed lower right, "Boccioni." Pencil, charcoal, blue and orange crayon, with gray wash on buff paper, $9^{1}/_{4} \times 18^{1}/_{2}$". Collection Mr. and Mrs. Harry Lewis Winston, Birmingham, Michigan. Ill. p. 38.

*25 *Mourning (Lutto)*, (1910). Oil on canvas, $41^{1}/_{2} \times 53$". Collection Mrs. Margarete Schultz, New York. Exhibited at the *Famiglia Artistica*, Milan, December 20–31, 1910. Ill. p. 39.

*26 *Riot in the Galleria (Rissa in Galleria)*. (1910). Oil on canvas, $30 \times 25^{1}/_{4}$". Collection Dr. Emilio Jesi, Milan. This painting is sometimes confused with the later work, *The Riot* (Cat. No. 34), and with *The Raid* in a private collection, Paris, for which two related drawings exist, dated April 1911, in the Marinetti Collection, Rome. Ill. p. 33.

27 Study for *The City Rises (Studio per La città sale)*. Signed lower right, "1910 U Boccioni." Crayon and chalk, $22^{1}/_{2} \times 33^{1}/_{2}$". Collection Estate of Vico Baer.

*28 Study for *The City Rises (Studio per La città sale)*. (1910–11). Oil on cardboard, $13 \times 18^{1}/_{2}$". Collection Dr. Gianni Mattioli, Milan. Ill. p. 36.

*29 Study for *The City Rises (Studio per La città sale)*. (1910–11). Signed lower right, "Boccioni." Tempera on paper, $14^{1}/_{8} \times 23^{5}/_{8}$". Collection Dr. Emilio Jesi, Milan. Ill. p. 36.

*30 *The City Rises (La città sale)*. (1910–11). Signed lower right, "U. Boccioni." Oil on canvas, $6' 6^{1}/_{2}" \times 9' 10^{1}/_{2}"$. The Museum of Modern Art, New York. Mrs. Simon Guggenheim Fund. (The left-hand third of this painting was partially damaged in the fire at the Museum of Modern Art on April 15, 1958. It has since been cleaned and restored.) Exhibited under the title *Lavoro (Work)* at *La Mostra d'Arte Libera* in the Padiglione Ricordi, Milan, April 30, 1911. It was shown also at the first Futurist exhibition in Paris February 1912, and subsequently in various countries. ". . . I have created a great synthesis of work, light and movement. It is possibly a transitional work *and I believe* one of the last." (Letter to Barbantini, Sept. 1910). Ill. p. 37.

*31 *Street Pavers (I selciatori)*. (1911). This painting has been dated variously but was probably executed during the summer of 1911. Oil on canvas, $39^{3}/_{8} \times 39^{3}/_{8}$". Collection Mr. and Mrs. Harry Lewis Winston, Birmingham, Michigan. Ill. p. 44.

32 *Modern Idol (Idolo moderno)*. (1911). Signed lower left, "Boccioni." Oil on canvas, $23^{1}/_{2} \times 23$". Collection Eric Estorick, London. Shown at *La Mostra d'Arte Libera*, Milan, April–May, 1911, at Bernheim-Jeune, Paris, 1912, and subsequent exhibitions.

*33 *The Laugh (La Risata).* (1911). Signed lower right, "U. Boccioni." Oil on canvas, $43^{3}/_{8} \times 57^{1}/_{4}$". The Museum of Modern Art, New York. Gift of Mr. and Mrs. Herbert M. Rothschild. According to Marinetti, the version of this painting exhibited at *La Mostra d'Arte Libera,* Milan, April–May 1911, was slashed with a razor. The present painting, which was shown in the first Futurist exhibition in Paris, February 1912, shows no evidence of this damage and was probably painted by Boccioni on his return from Paris in the late autumn of 1911. Ill. p. 40.

*34 *The Riot (Baruffa).* (1911). Signed lower right, "U. Boccioni." Oil on canvas, $19^{7}/_{8} \times 19^{7}/_{8}$". The Museum of Modern Art, New York. Given anonymously. Ill. p. 34.

*35 *Study of a Woman Surrounded by Houses* (Ines) *(Studio di donna tra case (Ines).* (1911). Oil on canvas, $53^{1}/_{8} \times 37$". Civica Galleria d'Arte Moderna, Milan. A preliminary drawing for this painting is on the back of a study for *The Farewells* (Cat. No. 36). Ill. p. 42.

36 *Study for States of Mind: The Farewells (Studio per Stati d'animo: Gli addii).* (1911). Signed lower right, "UB." Pencil, 19×24". Collection Mr. and Mrs. Harry Lewis Winston, Birmingham, Michigan. On the reverse is a preliminary drawing for *La Donna tra case.*

*37 *Study for States of Mind: The Farewells (Studio per Stati d'animo: Gli addii).* (1911). Signed lower right, "Boccioni." Pencil, 23×34". The Museum of Modern Art, New York. Gift of Vico Baer. Ill. p. 49.

*38 *States of Mind: The Farewells (Stati d'animo: Gli addii).* (1911). Oil on canvas, $27^{3}/_{4} \times 37^{7}/_{8}$". Collection Nelson A. Rockefeller, New York. This and the other two paintings of the triptych were shown at the Futurist exhibition at Bernheim-Jeune in February 1912, and subsequently in many European cities. This painting was normally exhibited between *Those Who Stay* and *Those Who Go.* Ill. p. 50.

*39 *Study for States of Mind: Those Who Stay (Studio per Stati d'animo: Quelli che restano).* (1911). Signed lower right, "Boccioni." Pencil, 23×24". The Museum of Modern Art, New York. Gift of Vico Baer. Ill. p. 48.

*40 *States of Mind: Those Who Stay (Stati d'animo: Quelli che restano).* (1911). Tempera and oil on canvas, $27^{7}/_{8} \times 37^{3}/_{4}$". Collection Nelson A. Rockefeller, New York. Ill. p. 51.

*41 *Study for States of Mind: Those Who Go (Studio per Stati d'animo: Quelli che vanno).* (1911). Signed lower right, "Boccioni." Pencil, 23×34". The Museum of Modern Art, New York. Gift of Vico Baer. Ill. p. 49.

*42 *States of Mind: Those Who Go (Stati d'animo: Quelli che vanno).* (1911). Oil on canvas, $27^{7}/_{8} \times 37^{3}/_{4}$". Collection Nelson A. Rockefeller, New York. The titles of the two paintings, *Those Who Go* and *Those Who Stay,* have sometimes been confused. Ill. p. 51.

*43 Drawing after *States of Mind: Those Who Stay (Disegno secondo Stati d'animo: Quelli che restano).* (1912). Ink, $12^{3}/_{4} \times 16^{3}/_{4}$". Collection Herbert and Nannette Roth-schild, Ossining, New York. Done after the painting, for reproduction in *Der Sturm.* Ill. p. 48.

*44 Drawing after *States of Mind: Those Who Go (Disegno secondo Stati d'animo: Quelli che vanno).* (1912). Ink, $12^{1}/_{2} \times 16^{3}/_{4}$". Collection Mr. and Mrs. Harry Lewis Winston, Birmingham, Michigan. Done after the painting, for reproduction in *Der Sturm.* Ill. p. 49.

*45 *Materia.* (1912). Oil on canvas, $7' \ 4^{3}/_{4}" \times 59^{1}/_{4}$". Collection Dr. Gianni Mattioli, Milan. This painting was shown at the Teatro Costanzi in Rome, February 1913, and later the same year in Rotterdam. In 1915 it was included in the Panama-Pacific International Exposition, San Francisco. It was reproduced in Boccioni's book, *Pittura, Scultura Futuriste,* 1914. The theme particularly interested Boccioni and he not only translated it into sculpture but later painted a more rhythmical version, *Horizontal Volumes* (Gall. Annunciata, Milan). Ill. p. 85.

46 *Study for Elasticity (Studio per Elasticità).* (1912). Signed upper right, "Boccioni" (on vertical). Pencil with gouache, $17^{1}/_{4} \times 17^{1}/_{4}$". The Museum of Modern Art, New York. Purchase.

*47 *Elasticity (Elasticità).* (1912). Oil on canvas, $39^{3}/_{8} \times 39^{3}/_{4}$". Collection Dr. Riccardo Jucker, Milan. Exhibited Rotterdam, 1913 and at the Panama-Pacific International Exposition, San Francisco, 1915. Ill. p. 88.

*48 *Anti-Graceful (The Artist's Mother) (Antigrazioso [La Madre]).* (1912). Bronze, 23" high. Collection Mr. and Mrs. Harry Lewis Winston, Birmingham, Michigan. This is the unique cast in bronze of the work. Ill. p. 91.

*49 *Development of a Bottle in Space (Sviluppo di una bottiglia nello spazio).* (1912). Bronze, 15" high. The Museum of Modern Art, New York. Aristide Maillol Fund. Exhibited at the Panama-Pacific International Exposition, San Francisco, 1915. Ill. p. 92.

*50 *Dynamism of a Soccer Player (Dinamismo di un footballer).* (1913). Oil on canvas, $6' \ 5" \times 6' \ 7$". Collection Mr. and Mrs. Sidney Janis, New York. Exhibited at the Panama-Pacific International Exposition, San Francisco, 1915. Ill. p. 89.

*51 *Muscular Dynamism (Dinamismo muscolare).* (1913). Signed lower right, "Boccioni." Charcoal, $34 \times 23^{1}/_{4}$". The Museum of Modern Art, New York. Purchase. Ill. p. 94.

*52 *Unique Forms of Continuity in Space (Forme uniche della continuità nello spazio).* (1913). Bronze, $43^{1}/_{2}$" high. The Museum of Modern Art, New York. Acquired through the Lillie P. Bliss Bequest. Four casts in bronze were made from the original plaster: two at an early date with polished surface (of which this is one), and two at a later date with the surface left closer to that of the plaster. Ill. p. 95.

*53 *Study for Dynamism of a Cyclist (Studio per Dinamismo di un ciclista).* (1913). Ink and ink wash, $8^{1}/_{4} \times 12^{3}/_{8}$". Yale University Art Gallery, New Haven. Collection Société Anonyme. Ill. p. 97.

*54 *Study for Dynamism of a Cyclist (Studio per Dinamismo di un ciclista).* (1913). Ink and tempera, $11^{1}/_{2} \times 15$". Civica Raccolta delle Stampe A. Bertarelli, Milan. Ill. p. 97.

*55 *Dynamism of a Cyclist (Dinamismo di un ciclista).*
(1913). Oil on canvas, 27½×37⅜". Collection Dr. Gianni
Mattioli, Milan. The painting was shown in the *Lacerba*
exhibition in Florence, November 30, 1913—January 15,
1914, and at the Panama-Pacific International Exposition, San Francisco, 1915. Ill. p. 96.

*56 *Dynamism of a Human Body (Dinamismo di un corpo
umano).* (1913–14). Oil on canvas, 39½×39½". Civica
Galleria d'Arte Moderna, Milan. This painting is closely
related to a drawing reproduced in *Lacerba* II, 6 (March
15, 1914), p. 89, entitled *I Want to Synthesize the Unique
Forms of Continuity in Space,* one of a series shown
with Boccioni's sculpture in Rome, December 1913. Ill.
p. 99.

57 *Plastic Dynamism, Horse and Houses (Dinamismo plastico, cavallo e case).* (1914). Signed lower right, "Boccioni" and inscribed "Dinamismo Plastico, Cavallo &
Case." Ink, 12⅝×16⅝" Collection Eric Estorick, London.

*58 *Plastic Dynamism: Horse + Rider + Houses (Dinamismo
plastico: cavallo + cavaliere + caseggiato).* (1914). Pencil,
ink, and watercolor, 15¼×22⅜". Civica Raccolta delle
Stampe A. Bertarelli, Milan. The drawing, which bears
the note "Studio per una scultura di materie diverse"
relates both to the sculpture in the Peggy Guggenheim
Collection, Venice, and several paintings of the same
subject. Ill. p. 100.

*59 *Plastic Dynamism: Horse + Houses (Dinamismo plastico:
cavallo + case).* (1914). Ink, watercolor, and gouache, 5¼
×8½". Civica Raccolta delle Stampe A. Bertarelli, Milan.
Ill. p. 100.

*60 *Horse + Rider + Houses (Cavallo + cavaliere + caseggiato).*
(1914). Signed lower right, "Boccioni." Oil on canvas,
41×52¾". Galleria Nazionale d'Arte Moderna, Rome.
Ill. p. 101.

*61 *Head of a Woman (Mother of the Artist?) (Testa di
donna [Madre dell'artista?]).* (1914). Signed lower right,
"Boccioni." Pencil, ink, and wash, 12×9½". Collection
Mr. and Mrs. Harry Lewis Winston, Birmingham, Michigan. Ill. p. 100.

*62 *"Scomposizione" of the Head of a Woman (Scomposi-
zione di testa di donna).* (1914). Tempera and collage
on canvas, 13¾×13¾". Civica Galleria d'Arte Moderna,
Milan. Ill. p. 100.

63 *"Scomposizione" of the Head of a Man (Scomposizione
di testa di uomo).* (1914). Tempera and collage on canvas,
13¾×13¾". Civica Galleria d'Arte Moderna, Milan.

64 Study for *The Drinker (Studio per Il Bevitore).* (1914).
Signed lower right, "Boccioni." Oil, gouache and collage,
11½×14½". Collection Mr. and Mrs. Harry Lewis Winston, Birmingham, Michigan.

*65 *The Drinker (Il Bevitore).* (1914). Signed lower left,
"U. Boccioni." Oil on canvas, 34¼×33⅞". Collection
Dr. Riccardo Jucker, Milan. Ill. p. 118.

*66 *The Cavalry Charge (Carica di lancieri).* (1914). Tempera and collage on cardboard, 12⅞×19½". Collection
Dr. Riccardo Jucker, Milan. (Reproduced in *Grande Illustrazione,* 13 (Jan. 1915), p. 4.) Ill. p. 114.

CARLO CARRÀ

Born Quargnento near Alessandria, Italy, February 1, 1881;
lives in Milan

Trained as a decorator in Milan, Carrà worked on decorations for the International Exposition in Paris in 1900
and later spent some time in London. In 1904 he attended the school of the Brera, studying with Cesare
Tallone, and in 1908 became active in the *Famiglia Artistica* in Milan. At this time he met Boccioni, Romani,
and Bonzagni with whom he signed the "Manifesto of
Futurist Painting." Very active in the movement until
1915, he then withdrew from the group around Marinetti. Meeting Giorgio de Chirico in a military hospital
in Ferrara in 1916, he joined with him in the movement
known as the *Scuola Metafisica,* for which he became
the most able theorist. He collaborated from 1919 to
1922 on the influential review *Valori Plastici,* and in
1924 became associated with the new group of figurative painters, the *Novecento.* He has written exten-
sively on art.

*67 *The Horsemen of the Apocalypse (I cavalieri dell'Apo-
calisse),* 1908. Signed lower right, "C. Carrà 908." Oil
on canvas, 14¼×37¼". Richard Feigen Gallery, Chicago. On the back is a note by Carrà stating that the
painting was awarded a prize at the *Famiglia Artistica* in 1908. Ill. p. 20.

*68 *The Swimmers (Nuotatrici).* Signed lower right, "C. D.
Carrà 1910." Oil on canvas, 41½×61¼". Carnegie Institute, Pittsburgh. Gift of G. David Thompson. The
painting was exhibited at *La Mostra d'Arte Libera,* Milan, April–May 1911, at the Bernheim-Jeune exhibition
in Paris in February 1912, and in later Futurist exhibitions. Ill. p. 29.

*69 *Leaving the Theater (Uscita da teatro).* (1910–11). Signed lower left. "C. D. Carrà." Oil on canvas, 23¾×
35½". Collection Eric Estorick, London. Carrà notes
in *La mia vita:* "This painting was suggested to me one
winter night while leaving the Teatro alla Scala ... I
believe that this canvas, completely ignored in Italy,
is one of the paintings in which I best expressed the
conception I then had of pictorial art. ..." p. 161. Exhibited at the Bernheim-Jeune exhibition, February
1912. Ill. p. 30.

*70 *Funeral of the Anarchist Galli (I funerali dell'anarchico
Galli).* (1910–11). Oil on canvas, 6' 6¼"×8' 6". The Museum of Modern Art, New York. Acquired through
the Lillie P. Bliss Bequest. This painting was shown
at *La Mostra d'Arte Libera,* Milan, April–May 1911, at
Bernheim-Jeune, Paris, in February 1912, and other
European galleries. It was one of the paintings sold
to Dr. Borchardt in Berlin in 1912. A note on the funeral (1904) that inspired the painting is in Carrà,
La mia vita, pp. 73–74. Ill. p. 31.

*71 *Jolts of a Cab (Sobbalzi di carrozzella).* (1911). Signed
lower right, "C. D. Carrà." Oil on canvas, 20⅝×26½".

Collection Herbert and Nannette Rothschild, Ossining, New York. Exhibited in the Bernheim-Jeune exhibition, Paris, February 1912, and in subsequent European group shows. Ill. p. 53.

*72 *What the Streetcar Said to Me* (Quello che mi disse il tram). (1911). Oil on canvas, 20^1/$_2$×27". Collection Dr. Giuseppe Bergamini, Milan. Exhibited in the Bernheim-Jeune exhibition, Paris, February 1912 and in subsequent group shows in Europe. Ill. p. 53.

*73 *Horse and Rider* (Cavallo e cavaliere). (1912). Signed upper right, "C. D. Carrà." Ink and watercolor, 10^1/$_4$× 14^1/$_4$". Collection Dr. Riccardo Jucker, Milan. This rather literal effort to demonstrate the statement in the Technical Manifesto, "... a horse in motion does not have four legs; it has twenty and their movements are triangular" has some stylistic elements in common with Severini's *Second Dancer*. Ill. p. 75.

*74 *Rhythms of Objects* (Ritmi di oggetti). (c. 1912). Oil on canvas, 20^1/$_8$×26". Collection Dr. Emilio Jesi, Milan. This painting was first exhibited at the Teatro Costanzi in Rome, February 1913. The signature and date lower left, "C. Carrà 911," were probably added later. Ill. p. 76.

75 Study for *The Galleria in Milan* (Studio per *La Galleria di Milano*). Signed lower left, "C. Carrà 1912." Pencil. Collection Dr. Gianni Mattioli, Milan.

*76 *The Galleria in Milan* (La Galleria di Milano). (1912). Oil on canvas, 36×20". Collection Dr. Gianni Mattioli, Milan. Ill. p. 77.

*77 *Study of a Female Nude*. Signed lower right, "Carrà 1912." Brush and ink, 32^1/$_4$×14^1/$_4$". Collection Dr. Emilio Jesi, Milan. This belongs to a series of studies of nudes in which Carrà developed the theory expressed in his article "Plastic Planes as Spherical Expansion in Space," *Lacerba*, I, 6 (March 15, 1913), pp. 53–55. Ill. p. 78.

78 *Dancer: Form in Circular Motion* (Danzatrice: Forma in moto circolare). (1912). Lower right, "Forma in moto circolare." Signed and dated 1910 lower left (although the drawing now bears the date 1910, it was more likely made in 1912). Charcoal. Collection Dr. Gianni Mattioli, Milan.

*79 *Boxer* (Composizione futurista). 1913. Signed lower right, "C. Carrà 913." Ink and ink wash, 9^5/$_8$×9^1/$_8$". Collection Mr. and Mrs. Joseph Slifka, New York. Ill. p. 79.

*80 *Boxer*. Signed lower right, "C. Carrà 1913." Ink, 23^5/$_8$× 19^5/$_8$". Collection Eric Estorick, London. Ill. p. 79.

*81 *"Free-Word" Painting (Patriotic Celebration)* (Dipinto parolibero [Festa patriotica]). (1914). Collage on cardboard, 15^1/$_8$×11^3/$_4$". Collection Dr. Gianni Mattioli, Milan. This "free-word" collage was reproduced in *Lacerba*, II, 15 (August 1, 1914), p. 233. Although it recently has been called *Manifesto for Intervention*, its title as given here was made specific in a letter from Marinetti to Soffici, July 21, 1914. *Archivi del Futurismo*, pp. 341–2. Ill. p. 111.

*82 *Pursuit* (Inseguimento). (1914). Collage and gouache, 15^1/$_4$×26^3/$_4$". Collection Dr. Gianni Mattioli, Milan. This work, with its obvious reference to the war, was reproduced in Carrà's *Guerrapittura*, 1915, p. 31. Ill. p. 112.

LEONARDO DUDREVILLE

Born Venice, April 4, 1885; lives in Ghiffa (Novara)

Although not a member of the Futurist group before the war, Dudreville, who helped to organize the *Nuove Tendenze* group in Milan in 1912, was strongly influenced by Futurist ideas, particularly those of Boccioni concerning the abstract expression of states of mind. He restated these convictions in the catalogue of the *Nuove Tendenze* exhibition of 1914, at which time he showed several of his non-objective paintings. Returning to figurative painting a few years after the war, he helped found the *Novecento* movement in 1924.

83 *Tragic Conflict* (Urto del Tragico). Signed lower right, "L. Dudreville 1913." Oil on canvas, 52×52". Collection N. Richard Miller, New York. Shown in the first exhibition of the *Nuove Tendenze* group, Milan, May–June 1914.

UGO GIANNATTASIO

Born Rome, August 2, 1888; died Turin, June 5, 1958

After studying with the sculptor Ximines and at the life classes of the academy in Rome, Giannattasio settled in Paris in 1909 where he knew Severini and other Italian and French artists associated with the new movements in art. Although he felt himself very much a Futurist painter, he did not exhibit under the Futurist banner until the "free" exhibition in Rome in 1914. A few years after the first World War, in which most of his works were destroyed, he largely gave up painting to travel and write. After the second World War in which he was for two years a prisoner of war in Germany, he returned to painting. His recent works were shown at the Cavallino Gallery in Venice in April 1958.

*84 *The Revolving Door of the Taverne de Paris* (Le Tourniquet de la Taverne de Paris). (1913). Oil on canvas, 64^1/$_2$×74^3/$_4$". Private collection, London. Exhibited at the Salon des Indépendants, Paris, 1913. Ill. p. 102.

OTTONE ROSAI

Born Florence, April 28, 1895; died Ivrea, May 13, 1957

Rosai studied in Florence where he had his first exhibition in 1913. Drawn to the Futurists, especially encouraged by Soffici, he exhibited in the Futurist show in Rome in 1914. His association with Futurism was brief; after the war he established his characteristic way of painting which he followed for the rest of his career.

*85 *The Carpenter's Bench (Il banco del falegname)*. Signed lower right, "O. Rosai 191(4?)". Oil and collage on cardboard, 18³/₄×27³/₄". Collection Dr. Emilio Jesi, Milan. Ill. p. 105.

LUIGI RUSSOLO

Born Portogruaro near Venice, May 1, 1885; died Cerro di Laveno on Lago Maggiore, February 4, 1947

Well schooled in music and self-trained in art, Russolo became associated with the Futurist group in Milan in 1909. He signed the "Manifesto of Futurist Painting" and participated actively in the movement, although much of his time from 1913 on was given to experiment with his *Intonarumori* (Noise Organ) on which he gave the first public concert at the Teatro Dal Verme, Milan, April 21, 1914. Volunteering for military service with other Futurists, he saw action on the Italian front and received a serious head wound that limited his later activity. Participating in the second phase of Futurism he painted little but gave much time to his concerts. When in 1941 he again devoted himself to painting, it was in a representational manner far from his Futurist work. His mystical ideas about life and art, much influenced by his later interest in Yoga, are expressed in his book, *Al di là della materia*, published in 1938.

*86 *Perfume (Profumo)*. (1909–10). Signed lower right, "L. Russolo." Oil on canvas, 25¹/₂×24³/₄". Collection Mr. and Mrs. Harry Lewis Winston, Birmingham, Michigan. Exhibited at *La Mostra Intima* of the *Famiglia Artistica*, Milan, December 21, 1910, and at *La Mostra d'Arte Libera*, Milan, April–May 1911. Ill. p. 27.

*87 *Music (La Musica)*. Signed lower right, "L. Russolo 1911." Oil on canvas, 7' 2"×55". Collection Eric Estorick, London. Exhibited at *La Mostra d'Arte Libera*, Milan, April–May 1911 and in Rome and Rotterdam in 1913. It was later called *Musical Dynamism*. Ill. p. 28.

*88 *Memories of a Night (Ricordi di una notte)*. (1911). Signed lower right, "L. Russolo." Oil on canvas, 39³/₄× 39³/₈". Collection Miss Barbara Jane Slifka, New York. Exhibited at Bernheim-Jeune, Paris, February 1912, and at other group showings throughout Europe. According to Severini it was painted after the trip to Paris in the autumn of 1911, but it shows no influence of Parisian painting. It is most closely related to some of Boccioni's paintings of 1911. Ill. p. 45.

*89 *The Revolt (La Rivolta)*. (1911). Oil on canvas, 59"× 7' 6¹/₂". Gemeente Museum, The Hague. This painting was exhibited at Bernheim-Jeune in February 1912 and in other European exhibitions. It was the painting by Russolo most commented on in the press. Ill. p. 52.

90 *Dynamism of an Automobile (Dinamismo di un automobile)*. Signed lower right, "L. Russolo 1911." Oil on canvas, 41×41". Musée National d'Art Moderne, Paris.

Exhibited at the *Lacerba* exhibition, Florence, December 1913.

*91 *Plastic Synthesis of the Actions of a Woman (Sintesi plastica dei movimenti di una donna)*. Signed lower right, "L. Russolo 1912." Oil on canvas, 33¹/₂×25¹/₂". Musée des Beaux Arts, Grenoble. The painting was exhibited in Rome at the Teatro Costanzi in February 1913, in Rotterdam the same year and at the Panama-Pacific International Exposition, San Francisco in 1915. Ill. p. 81.

*92 *The Solidity of Fog (Solidità della nebbia)*. Signed lower right, "L. Russolo 1912." Oil on canvas, 39¹/₄×25³/₄". Collection Dr. Gianni Mattioli, Milan. Exhibited at the Teatro Costanzi, Rome, February 1913 and later the same year in Rotterdam. Ill. p. 82.

ANTONIO SANT'ELIA

Born Como, April 30, 1888; killed in combat, October 10, 1916

After studying in Como, Sant'Elia established himself at Milan where he enrolled at the school of the Brera. He passed his architectural examinations at Bologna, then returned to Milan where he opened an office. In 1912 he joined in founding the group, *Nuove Tendenze*, and took part in the first exhibition of the group in May 1914. Later the same year he joined the Futurists, several of whom he had known for some time, and rewrote the preface to the May exhibition catalogue as the "Manifesto of Futurist Architecture."

93 Study for *The New City (Studio per La Città nuova)*. (1914). Ink, 14¹/₄×13³/₄". Collection Avv. Paride Accetti, Milan.

*94 *The New City (La Città nuova)*. Signed lower right, "Milano 1/3/1914 A. S." Ink with watercolor, 12¹/₄×6⁷/₈". Collection Avv. Paride Accetti, Milan. Ill. p. 107.

95 *The New City (La Città nuova)*. (1914). Ink and watercolor, 10⁵/₈×4³/₄". Collection Avv. Paride Accetti, Milan.

96 *The Power Plant (La Centrale elettrica)*. Dated lower right, "25/2/1914". Ink, pencil and watercolor, 11³/₄× 7⁷/₈". Collection Avv. Paride Accetti, Milan.

97 *The Power Plant (La Centrale elettrica)*. Signed and dated lower right, "Milano 15/3/1914 SE." Ink and watercolor, 11³/₄×7⁷/₈". Collection Avv. Paride Accetti, Milan.

GINO SEVERINI

Born Cortona, April 7, 1883; lives in Paris and Rome

Settling in Rome in 1899, Severini studied drawing at night and when possible attended the life classes of the academy. Later he studied, together with Boccioni, in Balla's studio. In the autumn of 1906 he settled in Paris, where he has worked chiefly ever since. He came to know Picasso, Braque, and many of the painters later associated with Cubism. Although he signed the "Manifesto of Futurist Painting," he had little direct association with the group in Milan until late in 1911. He did not take part in the Futurist theater presentations. In the 1920s he turned away from Futurism to a calmer figurative art based often on classical motifs.

*98 *Spring in Montmartre (Primavera a Montmartre).* 1909. Signed lower right, "G. Severini MCMIX." Oil on canvas, 28¼×23⅝". Private collection, Paris. Ill. p. 21.

*99 *The Boulevard (Le Boulevard).* (1910). Oil on canvas, 25⅛×36⅛". Collection Eric Estorick, London. Exhibited at Bernheim-Jeune, Paris, February 1912. Ill. p. 23.

*100 *The Modiste (La Modista).* (1910). Oil on canvas, 25⅜×18⅞". Collection Mr. and Mrs. Joseph Slifka, New York. According to Severini's recollection the work was painted at Civray in 1910. (Severini, *Tutta la vita di un pittore,* p. 74.) Ill. p. 47.

*101 *The Obsessive Dancer (Danzatrice Ossessionante).* (1911). Signed lower right, "G. Severini." Oil on canvas, 28¾×21⅝". Collection Mr. and Mrs. Samuel F. Kurzman, New York. Exhibited at Bernheim-Jeune, Paris, 1912 and reproduced in the catalogue. Ill. p. 47.

102 Study for *"Nord-Sud"* (1912). Charcoal, 17¾×21". Collection Herbert and Nannette Rothschild, Ossining, New York.

*103 *The "North-South" Métro (Nord-Sud).* Signed lower center, "1912 G. Severini." Oil on canvas, 19¼×25¼". Collection Dr. Emilio Jesi, Milan. Exhibited at the Marlborough Gallery, London, April 1913. It is discussed by the artist in his *Tutta la vita di un pittore,* p. 176. Ill. p. 72.

*104 *Self Portrait (Autoritratto).* (1912). Signed lower right, "G. Severini." Oil on canvas, 25¼×21⅝". Collection Dr. Giuseppe Sprovieri, Rome. This is probably the self portrait painted in 1912 and brought to Italy in the summer of that year by Severini. See Severini, *Tutta la vita* ... p. 157. Ill. p. 70.

105 Study for *Portrait of Mme M. S.* (Studio per *Ritratto della Signora M. S.*). Signed lower right, "G. Severini 1912." Pastel, 19¼×13⅞". Collection Mr. and Mrs. Harry Lewis Winston, Birmingham, Michigan.

*106 *Portrait of Mme M. S. (Ritratto della Signora M. S.).* (1912). Signed lower right, "G. Severini." Oil on canvas, 36¼×25½". Collection Mr. and Mrs. S. J. Zacks, Toronto. "Among these is an important portrait of Mme M. S. which shows my essentially plastic preoccupations. Was it in line with the Cubists or the Futurists? I confess that I was not concerned with the matter." Severini, *Tutta la vita* ... p. 153. Ill. p. 71.

*107 *The Blue Dancer (Ballerina bleu).* (1912). Oil on canvas, with sequins, 24⅛×18¼". Collection Dr. Gianni Mattioli, Milan. Exhibited in Rome and in Rotterdam in the spring of 1913. Ill. p. 2.

*108 *Second Dancer (White) (Seconda danzatrice [bianca]).* (1912). Oil on canvas, 23⅝×17¾". Collection Dr. Riccardo Jucker, Milan. This is probably one of the two paintings of dancers brought by Severini to Italy in the summer of 1912. Exhibited in Rome and in Rotterdam in the spring of 1913. Ill. p. 67.

109 *Dancers (Danzatrici).* (1912). Oil on canvas, 13½×10". Collection Mr. and Mrs. Sidney E. Cohn, New York.

*110 *Dynamic Hieroglyphic of the Bal Tabarin (Geroglifico dinamico del Bal Tabarin).* (1912). Oil on canvas, with sequins, 63⅝×61½". The Museum of Modern Art, New York. Acquired through the Lillie P. Bliss Bequest. Painted during the summer of 1912 in Pienza, Italy. Ill. p. 68.

111 *Dancer (Danzatrice).* Signed lower left, "G. Severini 1913." Oil on canvas, 39×30¾". Collection Mr. and Mrs. Morton G. Neumann, Chicago.

*112 *Dancer = Sea + Vase of Flowers (Ballerina = Mare + Vaso di fiori).* (1913). Signed lower right, "G. Severini." Oil on canvas, with aluminum, 36¼×23⅝". Collection Herbert and Nannette Rothschild, Ossining, New York. The concept underlying this painting is described by Severini in his essay "Le Analogie plastiche del dinamismo" written in 1913 but not published. See *Archivi del Futurismo,* pp. 76–80. Ill. p. 73.

113 Study for *Dancer = Sea* (Studio per *Danzatrice = Mare*). (1913). Signed lower right, "G. Severini." Charcoal, 27⅞×19⅞". Collection Mr. and Mrs. Harry Lewis Winston, Birmingham, Michigan.

*114 *Dancer = Sea (Danzatrice = Mare).* (1913–14). Signed lower right, "G. Severini." Oil on canvas, with sequins, 36½×28¾". Collection Mr. and Mrs. Harry Lewis Winston, Birmingham, Michigan. Ill. p. 73.

115 *Autobus.* Signed lower right, "G. Severini 1913." Charcoal, 21×18". Collection Miss May Walter, New York.

*116 *Spherical Expansion of Light (Centrifugal) (Espansione sferica della luce [centrifuga]).* (1914). Oil on canvas, 24⅜×19⅝". Collection Dr. Riccardo Jucker, Milan. The exact theory behind this painting is explained in Severini's "Le Analogie plastiche del dinamismo," 1913. See *Archivi del Futurismo,* pp. 76–80. Exhibited at the Panama-Pacific International Exposition, San Francisco, 1915. Ill. p. 74.

117 *War (Guerra).* (1915). Oil on canvas, 36¼×28¾". Collection Mr. and Mrs. Joseph Slifka, New York. This painting and those following concerned with the war were probably among those exhibited by the artist in Jan.–Feb. 1916 in his *Ire Exposition Futuriste d'Art Plastique de la Guerre,* La Galerie Boutet de Monvel, Paris.

*118 *The Armored Train (Il treno blindato).* (1915). Signed lower right, "G. Severini." Oil on canvas, 46×34½". Collection Richard S. Zeisler, New York. Ill. p. 115.

*119 *Flying over Reims.* (1915?). Charcoal, 22⅜×18⅝". The Metropolitan Museum of Art, New York. The Alfred Stieglitz Collection, 1949. Ill. p. 113.

MARIO SIRONI

Born Tempio Pausania (Sassari), May 12, 1885, of Milanese parents; lives in Milan

In Rome while studying mathematics at the University, Sironi met Boccioni, Severini, and Balla and became interested in painting. Although he maintained contact with Boccioni and expressed sympathy for the ideas of the Futurists, he first showed under the Futurist title at the "free" exhibition in Rome in 1914. In March 1915 he was officially made a part of the group. After the first World War his painting underwent a marked change, and in the early 1920s he helped to found the movement of the *Novecento*.

*120 *Self Portrait (Autoritratto)*. Signed lower left, "Sironi 1913." Oil on canvas, 20¼×19¼". Civica Galleria d'Arte Moderna, Milan. Ill. p. 103.

*121 *Composition with Propeller (Composizione con elica)*. (1915). Tempera and collage on cardboard, 29⅜×24¼". Collection Dr. Gianni Mattioli, Milan. Ill. p. 104.

*122 *Dancer (Ballerina)*. (1916). Collage, oil, and various media on canvas, 30×21⅝". Collection Dr. Riccardo Jucker, Milan. Ill. p. 104.

ARDENGO SOFFICI

Born Rignano sull'Arno, April 7, 1879; lives at Poggio a Caiano near Florence.

Having first studied painting in Florence, Soffici settled in Paris in 1900 and remained there until 1907, becoming familiar with all major trends in French painting and criticism. This knowledge gave his illuminating articles on modern art, written for *La Voce* on his return to Florence, particular importance. Although originally critical of the Futurist painters, he came to accept their ideas and became one of the group. *Lacerba*, which he founded with Giovanni Papini in 1913, was for some time the major outlet for Futurist writing. Towards the end of 1914 he cooled to the activity of the Futurists and in February 1915 publically separated himself from Marinetti's group. After the war he returned to a simple figurative style of painting.

*123 *Displacement of the Planes of a Lamp (Scomposizione dei piani di un lume)*. (1912). Oil on canvas, 13¾×11¾". Collection Eric Estorick, London. Exhibited at the Teatro Costanzi, Rome, February 1913, and in Rotterdam later the same year. Ill. p. 56.

*124 *Lines and Volumes of a Street (Linee e volumi di una strada)*. (1912). Oil on canvas, 20½×18½". Collection Dr. Riccardo Jucker, Milan. Exhibited at the Teatro Costanzi, Rome, February 1913, and in Rotterdam later the same year. Ill. p. 57.

125 *Interpenetration of Plastic Planes (Compenetrazione di piani plastici)*. (1913). Oil on canvas, 13⅜×9". Collection Dr. Giuseppe Bergamini, Milan.

126 *Futurist Landscape (Paesaggio futurista)*. (1913). Ink, 5½×7½". Collection Dr. Gianni Mattioli, Milan.

ADDENDA TO THE CATALOGUE

UMBERTO BOCCIONI

Woman Seated (Donna seduta). (1909). Oil and gouache on paper, 16½×11½". Collection Mr. and Mrs. Joseph Slifka, New York

At the Front (Paesaggio al Fronte). (1914). Ink, 8×8¼". Collection Dr. Gianni Mattioli, Milan

CARLO CARRÀ

Complementarism – Form – Nude. 1912. Oil and gouache on paper, 16½×11½". Inscribed and signed "*Complementarismo – forma – nudo/C. Carrà 912.*" Collection Mr. and Mrs. Joseph Slifka, New York

Index

by L. Lippard

Page numbers marked with an asterisk refer to illustrations